# READERS THEATER
## *for Building Fluency*

Strategies and Scripts for Making the Most of This Highly Effective, Motivating, and Research-Based Approach to Oral Reading

*By Jo Worthy*

New York • Toronto • London • Auckland • Sydney
Mexico City • New Delhi • Hong Kong • Buenos Aires

**Teaching** *Resources*

CREDITS:

Page 54: Excerpted from CINDER-ELLY by Frances Minters, copyright © 1994 by Frances Minters.
Used by permission of Viking Penguin, A Division of Penguin Young Readers Group,
A Member of Penguin Group (USA) Inc., 345 Hudson Street, NY, NY 10014. All rights reserved.

Page 54: Excerpted from THE JUDGE by Harve Zemach. Copyright © 1969 by Harve Zemach.
Published by Farrar, Straus and Giroux. All rights reserved.

Page 63: Adaptation of CATS THAT ROAR by Kimberly Weinberger. Copyright © 2002 by Scholastic Inc.
Reprinted by permission.

Page 73: Cover of THE GREAT KAPOK TREE by Lynne Cherry. Copyright © 1990 by Lynne Cherry.
Published by Harcourt Inc.

Page 79: Used by permission of Curtis Brown, Ltd. from *The Boy Who Cried Wolf* by Freya Littledale.
Copyright © 1975 by Freya Littledale. All rights reserved.

Page 82: Based on the book *Los Tres Cerdos/The Three Pigs: Nacho, Tito, and Miguel* by Bobbi Salinas.
Copyright © 1998 by Piñata Publications. Adapted with permission of Piñata Publications.

Page 85: "Fox Escapes," "Fox in Charge," "Fox on Stage," from *Fox at School* by Edward Marshall,
copyright © 1983 by Edward Marshall. Used by permission of Dial Books for Young Readers,
a division of Penguin Young Readers Group, a member of Penguin Group (USA) Inc.,
345 Hudson Street, New York, NY 10014. All rights reserved.

Page 91: Adapted by permission of Scholastic Inc. from *The Librarian from the Black Lagoon* by Mike Thaler.
Copyright © 1997 by Mike Thaler.

Page 94: Used by permission of HarperCollins Publishers from *Sheila Rae, the Brave* by Kevin Henkes.
Copyright © 1987 by Kevin Henkes.

Page 97: Used by permission of HarperCollins Publishers from *The Little Old Lady Who Was Not Afraid of
Anything* by Linda Williams. Text copyright © 1986 by Linda D. Williams.

Page 102: Adaptation based on *Micro Monsters: Life Under the Microscope by* Christopher Maynard. Dorling
Kindersley Publishing, a division of Penguin Group UK Ltd.

Page 106: Used by permission of Children's Press/Franklin Watts, a Scholastic Library
Publishing Company, Inc., from *How to Eat Fried Worms* by Thomas Rockwell.
Text copyright © 1973 by Thomas Rockwell.

Every effort has been made to acquire permission to use the materials in this book.

Cover design by Maria Lilja.
Interior design by Solutions by Design, Inc.
Cover photos, clockwise from top left, courtesy of the author;
© Jeff Greenberg/PhotoEdit; © Bob Daemmrich/The Image Works.
Interior photos courtesy of Kathleen McDonnold and the author.

ISBN 0-439-52223-4

Copyright © 2005 by Jo Worthy

3  4  5  6  7  8  9  10      40    12  11  10  09  08  07

# Table of Contents

**Introduction** .................................................. 9

   Why I Wrote This Book ........................................ 9

   My Personal Background and Experience With Readers Theater ......... 9

   How This Book Is Organized .................................. 10

CHAPTER 1

**What Is Readers Theater and What Are Its Benefits?** ............ 11

   **What Is Readers Theater?** ................................... 12

      A Proven Instructional Approach (or What to Tell Your Principal) .......... 12

   **What Are the Benefits of Readers Theater?** ..................... 14

      Provides an Inclusive Alternative to the Traditional School Play .......... 14

      Allows You to Group by Interest Rather Than Ability ................. 15

      Connects Students to Real Literature ............................ 15

      Enhances Comprehension ..................................... 16

      Fosters Fluency ............................................. 17

      Builds Writing Skills ......................................... 17

      Brings Together Many Aspects of Literacy ........................ 19

      Can Be Used Across the Curriculum ............................. 19

      Reaches a Range of Students ................................... 19

   **Final Thought** ............................................ 24

CHAPTER 2

**Readers Theater Develops Fluency** ........................... 25

   **What Is Reading Fluency and Why Is It Important?** ............... 26

   **How Fluent Reading Develops** ................................ 26

   **Repeated Reading** .......................................... 27

   **The Problems With Using Repeated Reading Alone** ................ 28

      Students Complain, "We Already Read It!" ........................ 28

      Practice Without Performance Can Wear Thin ..................... 29

      Repeated Reading Does Not Specifically Address Comprehension and Interpretation .......... 29

Why Readers Theater Is a Better Choice for Improving Fluency. . . . . . . . . . . . . . . . . . . . 30

Final Thought. . . . . . . . . . . . . . . . . . . . . . . . . . . . . . . . . . . . . . . . . . . . . . . . . . . . . . . 31

CHAPTER 3

**Getting Organized and Setting the Stage**. . . . . . . . . . . . . . . . . . . . . . . . . . . . . . . . 33

**Supplies**. . . . . . . . . . . . . . . . . . . . . . . . . . . . . . . . . . . . . . . . . . . . . . . . . . . . . . . . . . 34

Scripts. . . . . . . . . . . . . . . . . . . . . . . . . . . . . . . . . . . . . . . . . . . . . . . . . . . . . . . . . . . 34

Costumes and Props. . . . . . . . . . . . . . . . . . . . . . . . . . . . . . . . . . . . . . . . . . . . . . . 35

Organizing Supplies. . . . . . . . . . . . . . . . . . . . . . . . . . . . . . . . . . . . . . . . . . . . . . . 36

**Getting Started: Lessons to Introduce Readers Theater**. . . . . . . . . . . . . . . . . . . . . 37

Introduction Lesson. . . . . . . . . . . . . . . . . . . . . . . . . . . . . . . . . . . . . . . . . . . . . . . 37

Review Lesson. . . . . . . . . . . . . . . . . . . . . . . . . . . . . . . . . . . . . . . . . . . . . . . . . . . 40

Transition Lesson. . . . . . . . . . . . . . . . . . . . . . . . . . . . . . . . . . . . . . . . . . . . . . . . . 42

**Incorporating Readers Theater Into Your Language Arts Program**. . . . . . . . . . . . . 44

Basic Practice and Performance Schedules. . . . . . . . . . . . . . . . . . . . . . . . . . . . . . 44

Variations on Basic Schedules. . . . . . . . . . . . . . . . . . . . . . . . . . . . . . . . . . . . . . . 47

**Final Thought**. . . . . . . . . . . . . . . . . . . . . . . . . . . . . . . . . . . . . . . . . . . . . . . . . . . . . . 48

CHAPTER 4

**Finding and Creating Scripts for Readers Theater**. . . . . . . . . . . . . . . . . . . . . . . . 49

**Using Performance-Ready Scripts**. . . . . . . . . . . . . . . . . . . . . . . . . . . . . . . . . . . . . 51

Internet Resources. . . . . . . . . . . . . . . . . . . . . . . . . . . . . . . . . . . . . . . . . . . . . . . . 51

Commercial Collections. . . . . . . . . . . . . . . . . . . . . . . . . . . . . . . . . . . . . . . . . . . . 51

Children's Books. . . . . . . . . . . . . . . . . . . . . . . . . . . . . . . . . . . . . . . . . . . . . . . . . 52

**Scripting Children's Literature**. . . . . . . . . . . . . . . . . . . . . . . . . . . . . . . . . . . . . . . . 55

Book Choice. . . . . . . . . . . . . . . . . . . . . . . . . . . . . . . . . . . . . . . . . . . . . . . . . . . . 55

Script Length. . . . . . . . . . . . . . . . . . . . . . . . . . . . . . . . . . . . . . . . . . . . . . . . . . . 56

Quality Control. . . . . . . . . . . . . . . . . . . . . . . . . . . . . . . . . . . . . . . . . . . . . . . . . . 56

**Guidelines for Adapting Different Kinds of Books**. . . . . . . . . . . . . . . . . . . . . . . . . 56

Series Books. . . . . . . . . . . . . . . . . . . . . . . . . . . . . . . . . . . . . . . . . . . . . . . . . . . . 56

Fairy Tales, Transformations, and Variants. . . . . . . . . . . . . . . . . . . . . . . . . . . . . . 59

More Complex Adaptations. . . . . . . . . . . . . . . . . . . . . . . . . . . . . . . . . . . . . . . . . 59

**Having Students Write Scripts**. . . . . . . . . . . . . . . . . . . . . . . . . . . . . . . . . . . . . . . . 63

Introductory Writing Lesson. . . . . . . . . . . . . . . . . . . . . . . . . . . . . . . . . . . . . . . . . 65

Writing Scripts with Less Teacher Support. . . . . . . . . . . . . . . . . . . . . . . . . . . . . . 67

**Final Thought**. . . . . . . . . . . . . . . . . . . . . . . . . . . . . . . . . . . . . . . . . . . . . . . . . . . . . . 68

CHAPTER 5
## Preparing for and Carrying Out Performances for a Real Audience ......... 69

Inviting Audience Members and Establishing the Program ....................... 70

Invitations to the Performance ............................................... 70

Programs for the Performance ............................................... 70

Selecting Scripts ............................................................. 71

Reviewing Responsibilities of Performers and Audience Members ................... 72

Performers ................................................................. 73

Audience Members .......................................................... 74

Performance Day ............................................................. 74

Final Thought ............................................................... 74

## Closing Thoughts ........................................................... 75

## Appendix: Scripts ........................................................... 77

*The Boy Who Cried Wolf* (Freya Littledale, 1987) ................................. 79

*Los Tres Cerdos/The Three Little Pigs: Nacho, Tito, and Miguel* (Bobbi Salinas, 1998) ....... 82

"Fox in Charge," "Fox Escapes," and "Fox on Stage" from
*Fox at School* (Edward Marshall, 1983) ......................................... 85

*The Librarian From the Black Lagoon* (Mike Thaler, 1997) ......................... 91

*Sheila Rae, the Brave* (Kevin Henkes, 1996) ..................................... 94

*The Little Old Lady Who Was Not Afraid of Anything* (Linda Williams, 2002) ........... 97

"Mighty Mites" and "Billions of Bacteria" from *Micro Monsters: Life Under the Microscope*
(Christopher Maynard, 1999) ................................................. 102

"The Bet" from *How to Eat Fried Worms* (Rockwell, 1973) ......................... 106

## Professional References Cited ............................................... 109

## Selected Children's Books Cited ............................................. 111

# Dedication

*This book is dedicated with all my love
to Don, Jared, Jenna, and Phoebe*

# Acknowledgments

I am grateful to many friends and colleagues who contributed ideas and inspiration for this book. The students, faculty, and parents of Allison Elementary School in Austin, Texas, provided enthusiasm, emotional support, teaching ideas, and a wonderful forum for trying out Readers Theater scripts and performances. Thank you to everyone who cheered on the students at Readers Theater productions. I am so privileged to be a part of your community. Marilyn Elrod, Allison's guardian angel, has been a constant source of inspiration and encouragement. You are my hero.

The practicing and future teachers who have participated in the "Reading Club" over the years have contributed ideas for scripts and performances, along with great passion for helping children love reading. Carol Bedard and Kathleen McDonnold opened their classrooms so I could observe their brilliant Readers Theater teaching, practice, and student productions. Finally, my buddies who love Readers Theater have provided an endless source of inspiration with creative scripts and classroom stories. Heartfelt thanks to Susan Buchanan, Denise Duncan, Bonnie Elliott, Rosemary Flores, Michelle Horsey, Beth Patterson, Kathryn Prater, Sheryl Prater, Nancy Roser, Misty Sailors, and Margo Turner.

And to Jason Buckingham, first-grade teacher at Allison Elementary School, and to Gay Ivey, Associate Professor at James Madison University, an extra-special thanks. Their scripts appear in the Appendix and are an important contribution to this book.

Many thanks, too, to the teachers and students (and to the parents of the students) whose photographs appear in the book. Photographs were taken at Lakeway, Allison, and Doss Elementary Schools in Austin, Texas.

I'd also like to thank the editors at Scholastic Books. Terry Cooper, Editor-in-Chief, Teaching Resources, and Joanna Davis-Swing, Executive Editor, supported this project through its publication. Merryl Maleska Wilbur, production and project editor, monitored and managed details attentively and gave a great deal of time and care to this book. Most of all I'd like to thank my development editor, Ray Coutu, who was there from start to finish, helping me to originate the project and shape the ideas, always pushing me gently to make it better. Thanks to all of you for making this book happen.

# Introduction

Friday has finally arrived, and Mr. Raymond's fourth graders are ready. All week they have been practicing their parts for their Readers Theater performance of *Cinder-Elly* (Minters, 1997), a modern version of Cinderella, and they can hardly contain their excitement as their families walk in and sit in the rows of chairs set up in the back of the classroom. "Here they come," whispers Aisha. Ronnie nods his head, smiles, and reads over his part one more time. After everyone is seated, Mr. Raymond announces the first performance and the players file onto the makeshift stage at the front of the room. Ana, a painfully shy student who struggles with reading, has her first starring role as the title character. Tears in his eyes, Ana's father watches and listens in amazement as she "becomes" the character and then receives the first standing ovation of her life.

## Why I Wrote This Book

Reading has been a hot topic in U.S. politics and media for many years. Our nation's economic and intellectual health has for years been linked to the national literacy rate. More recently, we have heard about the importance of using research-based practices to teach reading and writing. I wrote this book because I want to spread the news about Readers Theater, an activity that combines research-based reading instruction with a fun, exciting experience that even the most resistant students want to do again and again. Further, as I will explain in upcoming chapters, Readers Theater goes beyond reading instruction to address all aspects of literacy learning and even learning in the content areas. I want every teacher and student to have the opportunity to participate in Readers Theater.

## My Personal Background and Experience With Readers Theater

Knowing the connection between time spent reading and academic progress, I strive in my career to find ways to "turn on" students to reading. In my years as an elementary and middle school teacher, a professor of reading methods in a teacher preparation program, and the mother of a resistant reader (Worthy, 1998), the single most motivating activity I have ever found is Readers Theater. When I work with school faculties on professional development, I present a wide range of instructional activities, and teachers are interested in many of them. But, without fail, Readers Theater is the approach that captivates everyone.

I usually introduce Readers Theater by having the teachers practice and perform scripts for their colleagues in small groups amid lots of laughter and applause. I then give teachers several scripts to try with their students, and we meet again to share these experiences.

There are always a few teachers who leave the first meeting convinced that their students won't participate in or enjoy Readers Theater. They wonder particularly about the students who are shy or don't like reading out loud. These are valid concerns that I will discuss later. However, without fail, when we reconvene, even those teachers bring success stories. For example, a fourth-grade special education teacher shared that her students were thrilled with Readers Theater, worked cooperatively during their practice (requiring very few directions), and asked to perform for the whole school. A fifth-grade language arts teacher attributed her students' improved achievement to the increased time they spent reading and talking about books during Readers Theater units. I hear again and again about the incredible difference that Readers Theater makes for all students. Teachers tell me about:

⊙ The shy student who turned into a ham when he performed in front of the class.

⊙ The student who struggled with her part but, after practicing it at home, read it like an expert.

⊙ The student who never participated in anything but soon became a Readers Theater fanatic.

⊙ The outsider who learned to work productively with peers.

⊙ The student who performed poorly on achievement tests but whose scores improved over time, thanks in large part to Readers Theater.

⊙ The student who showed up one day with a Readers Theater script that she had written spontaneously at home. (This has happened to me many times.)

⊙ The many students who beg to "do it again."

The first few times I conducted these workshops, I was a little taken aback by the excitement generated by Readers Theater. Now, I expect it. Readers Theater is a transforming experience. It not only addresses reading fluency, interest, and comprehension; it pulls in even the most resistant readers, and it gives students a productive way to work together toward a common goal.

# How This Book Is Organized

In the first chapter of this book, I describe Readers Theater and discuss its many benefits. In Chapter 2, I explain reading fluency, an important reading skill that Readers Theater addresses. I talk about traditional methods of fluency instruction and why Readers Theater is a better way to focus on this essential aspect of reading instruction. In Chapter 3, I discuss how to get started with Readers Theater, with recommendations for gathering and organizing materials, step-by-step lessons for introducing Readers Theater, and suggested schedules. Chapter 4 focuses on scripts for Readers Theater—where to get them, how to write them, and how to help students write their own scripts. In Chapter 5, I address how to prepare for performances. Throughout the book, I include anecdotes and photographs gathered from my visits with teachers and students as they use Readers Theater in their classrooms. In the Appendix, I provide original scripts of "real" books that can be copied and used with your class.

# Chapter 1

# What Is Readers Theater and What Are Its Benefits?

Maybe you're a new teacher; maybe you've been teaching for 35 years; perhaps you're somewhere in between. Maybe you've never heard of Readers Theater; maybe you've been using it for years; perhaps you've always meant to try it. Maybe your students are all thriving, avid readers; maybe you couldn't make your students pick up a book if you gave them a million dollars; probably your students run the gamut. No matter what your situation, I think you will find something in this book that will make you want to try Readers Theater and/or experiment with new approaches and materials.

In this chapter, you'll find an overview of Readers Theater and an outline of the steps it involves. You'll also read about the many, wide-ranging benefits of Readers Theater with examples from real classrooms, and you'll almost certainly recognize some of your students in the examples.

# What Is Readers Theater?

Readers Theater is an instructional approach in which students read a book (or hear a book read aloud) and then perform a play (the book written in script form) by reading the script aloud to an audience. Readers Theater differs from other kinds of performances in that participants *read* rather than memorize their parts. As Sam Sebesta, former teacher and teacher educator says:

> Readers Theater introduces the element of drama into literacy learning and magically transforms the classroom into a stage. During Readers Theater time, the reader is at center stage, totally absorbed in reading. The reader is a star. (Sebesta, 2003)

Participants portray characters and events by using their voices expressively, rather than by relying on elaborate costumes or stage sets, so Readers Theater requires little advance planning when it comes to materials. According to Aaron Shepard (2003), a children's author and Readers Theater aficionado, the technique was originally used in colleges as a way of presenting literature in dramatic form. It has gradually made its way to earlier grades, where it has also been shown to be a highly motivating approach to reading. Shepard says:

> Kids love to do it, and they give it their all—more so because it's a team effort, and they don't want to let down their friends! And if the script is based on an available book, they of course all want to read it.

Box 1-1 explains the basic steps of Readers Theater and the learning benefits of each step. I explore these steps in more detail in later chapters.

## A PROVEN INSTRUCTIONAL APPROACH (OR WHAT TO TELL YOUR PRINCIPAL)

In the past few years, the term "research-based practices" has worked its way into everyday language. Readers Theater fits the research-based agenda in many ways. First, it is built on the strategy of repeated reading, which improves reading fluency, an essential aspect of reading and a major focus of state and national standards for reading (Carver & Hoffman, 1981; Strecker, Roser, & Martinez, 1999; Samuels, 1994). Unlike repeated reading, however, Readers Theater has an authentic communication purpose—to present a piece of literature to an audience—and thus provides students with a motivation for repeated reading (Rinehart, 1999). At the same time, Readers Theater provides an active, analytical framework for reading and helps students to understand and interpret what they read (Wolf 1993; 1998).

It's the quintessential, flexible, multidimensional approach to reading and writing. Effective performances are built upon positive social interactions focused on reading and writing, in which modeling, instruction, and feedback are natural components of rehearsals. Even resistant readers eagerly engage in practicing for Readers Theater performance, reading and rereading scripts many times (Tyler & Chard, 2000). Thus, Readers Theater is not just an effective instructional method; it's an activity that teachers and students—even students in the intermediate grades—become passionate about. Teachers can feel confident about using Readers Theater, both because it is grounded in research and because it is motivating and engaging. In the next section, I describe some of the benefits of using Readers Theater.

Box 1-1

# Basic Steps of Readers Theater

1. *Teacher reads aloud the book upon which the script is based* (promotes fluency, vocabulary development, comprehension, literature appreciation). To develop fluency, students need to hear many examples of fluent speaking and reading. During the read aloud, students hear a model of fluent reading and have the opportunity to use comprehension strategies and learn new vocabulary as they discuss and respond to the content of the book.

2. *Students read the script independently while the teacher gives feedback* (promotes fluency, decoding and word identification, vocabulary development, enhanced comprehension). When students read scripts independently, they have the opportunity to focus more closely on the text, to practice word identification and comprehension strategies in a text they have already heard, and to see new vocabulary words in context.

3. *Students practice their scripts in groups* (promotes fluency, enhanced comprehension, working in groups). After reading their scripts with the teacher's help, students practice reading in groups. Their accuracy and fluency improve with each reading because they are practicing and receiving teacher feedback. As students' reading becomes more automatic, they are able to focus on how to interpret their parts for an audience, thus enhancing their comprehension. They refer to the book as they decide how to read and act out their parts.

4. *Students prepare for performances* (promotes fluency, literature interpretation, working in groups, public speaking). As students get ready for performances, they have the opportunity to interact productively with their peers as they work together to prepare a presentation that will be interesting and understandable for their audience. They are motivated to read and reread so their performance will be a success. As they decide how to use their voices and actions, they are using higher-level comprehension skills to interpret characters and story events.

5. *Teachers and students evaluate reading, writing, and performances* (promotes assessment and self-assessment). Readers Theater offers many opportunities for teachers and students to continuously evaluate their learning and progress in each of the areas listed above.

6. *Students write scripts* (promotes enhanced comprehension, writing skills). After students have had experience performing prepared scripts, many teachers support students in writing scripts. When students write their own scripts, they gain practice in judging what it takes to make a script understandable to an audience.

# What Are the Benefits of Readers Theater?

There are many benefits to making Readers Theater a regular part of your language arts program. Here, I explain some of them. Throughout this section, I introduce a number of teachers and students through both anecdotes and photographs. During my visits to schools and as part of my workshops, I had the privilege of meeting with these teachers and students and hearing about and observing Readers Theater in action in their classrooms.

## PROVIDES AN INCLUSIVE ALTERNATIVE TO THE TRADITIONAL SCHOOL PLAY

Many schools have end-of-year, grade-level plays. Teachers and students spend a great deal of time on these productions, making costumes and sets, memorizing lines, and rehearsing. Although such performances can be wonderful experiences for everyone involved, they do not provide equal benefits for every student. Because they must learn and memorize many lines, the students who are chosen for lead parts are usually skilled readers and outgoing. Students with academic challenges and those who are shy are typically given smaller roles or non-speaking parts, such as stagehands or scenery builders.

I speak from experience. During my first year of teaching fifth grade, the three classes of students were grouped homogeneously according to their performance on achievement tests. I taught the class with the poorest scores, known throughout the school as "the low group." Each year, the three fifth-grade classes spent the last two months of school rehearsing a play to be presented for the community. Our play was about legendary football coach Knute Rockne (who, by the way, none of the students had ever heard of).

Students in the three classes auditioned for speaking parts, and my students and I were very disappointed to learn that not a single student from our class was chosen. A few volunteered to be stagehands, several had one or two lines as part of a crowd of football fans, but most of my students had no responsibilities for the play except to sit in the bleachers and be "faces in the crowd." Yet, every student in every class was expected to attend rehearsals, which were held during and after school for two hours a day. Most of my students sat backstage doing nothing during rehearsals.

My disappointment turned to anger as I thought about the waste of instructional time, not to mention the snub to my students, who I knew were very capable of handling speaking parts in the play. But I was the newest and most inexperienced teacher in the fifth grade, so I said nothing. That was more than 20 years ago, and I still get angry when I think about it. If I could relive that time, I would insist on

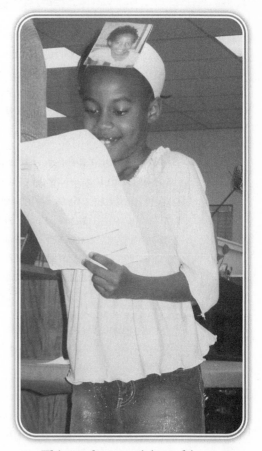

*This student participated in a semester-long, after-school tutoring program for reading. At the end-of-program performance party, she starred in a production of Doreen Cronin's* Click, Clack, Moo: Cows That Type *with her proud mother and grandmother in the audience.*

changing those traditional practices that were not only a waste of time but, I believe, harmful to my students' academic progress and sense of self worth. I would use Readers Theater instead and give my students the opportunity to be in multiple performances throughout the year—first in the safe, low-key setting of the classroom and then in front of other audiences.

Further, unlike elaborate one-time-only performances, Readers Theater can be a regular instructional activity. When we weave Readers Theater into the language arts program, we give all students the opportunity to practice with teacher support, to successfully perform their parts, and to increase their self-confidence (Measley, 1990). These opportunities lead to improved reading and thinking. Thus, Readers Theater is especially beneficial for challenged readers. When we use Readers Theater scripts of books that interest students instead of a published play we chose, we also make the experience more relevant and engaging. Readers Theater gives all students the option, opportunity, and motivation to participate in performances.

## ALLOWS YOU TO GROUP BY INTEREST RATHER THAN ABILITY

One of the most wonderful things about Readers Theater is that it is a perfect multilevel activity (Cunningham & Allington, 2003) that allows teachers to group students heterogeneously rather than by ability, as is often done in "reading groups." Because the level of difficulty of different parts within a script can vary widely, students can be grouped by interest and choice rather than by reading level. Students can take parts that provide just the right amount of challenge and support, or they can take more difficult parts if they choose to practice at home or read with a partner.

Of course, you will not give students reading material that is far beyond their reading skills. However, there are several sources of built-in support in Readers Theater that make it possible for a student to read material that might otherwise be considered too challenging. First and most important is the fact that students are never asked to read their scripts "cold." In Readers Theater, students are always familiar with the book on which the script is based because the teacher reads it aloud or students read it themselves; they have heard the words before they even see the script. Additionally, students are given copies of the script to read on their own at school and/or at home before they get together with their groups to rehearse. Those students who need extra help can get it from the teacher or their parents before they begin group rehearsals. So teachers can use different grouping formats, based on students' interests, group dynamics, or even random assignment, giving students the opportunity to work with different classmates. Students who struggle with reading need models of fluent reading, and they need challenges to build confidence.

## CONNECTS STUDENTS TO REAL LITERATURE

Readers Theater exposes students to high-quality children's literature because scripts are usually based on that literature. Several Web sites offer free scripts, and there are many books of plays available for sale. However, because of copyright laws, Readers Theater scripts based on real books can't be legally shared without permission. The publisher of this book, Scholastic, agreed to secure permission from the authors and publishers of real children's literature so I could write scripts and include them in this book. (See Appendix.)

Why is this important? One of the most exciting benefits of Readers Theater is that students almost always want to read the books that are performed. If these are real books that are in the library, students will line up to check them out and read them. That's why I felt so strongly about including scripts from real books. It's also a great reason to write your own scripts based on books that you have in your classroom—books that you know students will enjoy and that are aligned with your curriculum. With the suggestions and models provided here, students can also write their own scripts based on books they are reading. Teachers and students can share scripts they have written. The possibilities are limitless.

## ENHANCES COMPREHENSION

There's nothing more important in reading than comprehension, because the goal of reading is making meaning. Without comprehension, reading is only pronouncing words. Yet, in some classroom reading activities, it's sometimes hard to be sure that students are truly comprehending what they read. In Readers Theater, students read and discuss books and scripts many times to make their performances understandable to their audience. To be able to interpret events and character motives in their performances, students need a deep understanding of what they read. As a result, the quality of their understanding will be evident; you won't need to ask them comprehension questions to determine it.

*Preparing to read a book or script out loud to an audience is a wonderful way to work on fluency and comprehension.*

Mrs. Singh, a third-grade teacher, had built an impressive collection of Readers Theater scripts focused on traditional fairy tales and fairy tale "transformations" (e.g., Jon Scieszka's *The True Story of the Three Little Pigs* and Frances Minters's *Cinder-Elly*). She started the year with the traditional stories and worked her way through the transformations. She always read the stories aloud to the class at the beginning of each week and let students choose the script they wanted to perform. Students then worked in groups to rehearse their stories for a Friday "performance party." One week, each group was doing a different transformation of *The Three Little Pigs*. As she moved from group to group to give students support and feedback, Mrs. Singh realized that one group of students did not fully understand the subtleties of the story they were reading. She recalled:

> Even though I had read the story aloud and we had discussed it before
> handing out the scripts, it became clear during the rehearsals that they
> had missed some of the humor and irony in the story. As they were
> discussing what kind of voice expression to use and what kinds of
> costumes to make, they realized that they didn't understand a crucial part
> of the story, and they knew that the audience wouldn't get it if they
> didn't. They asked to see the book so they could reread the parts they were
> unsure about. It really opened my eyes to the fact that comprehension is
> such an active process and sometimes you have to really dig in to get the
> deep meaning.

## FOSTERS FLUENCY

Although Readers Theater is a multidimensional approach, many reading educators think of it primarily as a tool for developing reading fluency. Fluent readers can read and comprehend efficiently and with appropriate expression. Without fluency, students have trouble keeping up with their schoolwork and they often fall behind in school and become less motivated to read. In Chapter 2, I explain fluency, describe traditional methods of fluency instruction, and show how Readers Theater is an excellent way to build on traditional methods.

## BUILDS WRITING SKILLS

Readers Theater enhances writing skills by exposing students to well-written children's literature. As they listen to books, practice, and perform scripts, they are constantly seeing models of the kind of writing that entices readers and listeners. When students adapt books and write original scripts, they are writing for a real audience. With experience, students learn that they need to write thoughtfully and revise carefully in order to hold their audience's attention.

As an experienced fifth-grade teacher, Carol Bedard was always "on the lookout" for ways she could help her students make their writing more comprehensible. They tended to omit important details and other essential information in their personal writing. Conversely, they sometimes gave so much information that the reader got bogged down in the details. Indeed, these are challenges that all writers face. Mrs. Bedard has used Writers Workshop in her classroom for many years, but she wanted to take her students a step further. She describes it this way: "I hit the jackpot when I began having my students develop Readers Theater scripts in groups."

Mrs. Bedard's students had performed Readers Theater many times, but they had never written scripts. She found a Web site with a script of a scene from the first chapter of *When Zachary Beaver Came to Town* (Holt, 1999) at http://www.suzyred.com/ 2001zachtheater.html. She downloaded the script and had students practice it in groups and perform it for the class. Next, she let them try writing their own scripts. First, they independently read the first two chapters of the novel. Then, working in groups, the students wrote summaries, which they turned into Readers Theater scripts. Mrs. Bedard gave them 30 minutes of class time to write the scripts. She was amused when some of her reluctant writers complained that they did not have enough time to write their scripts. And she was amazed when "Several groups came in at lunch to work on the project, and one group gathered

*These students are collaborating on a Readers Theater script based on a novel they have read. This process enhances their reading, their writing, and their ability to work together, while giving them the opportunity to think deeply about literature.*

at a group member's home to work on the script. One girl took her group's script home, typed it, and made several revisions."

Each group performed their script for the class. After the performances, Mrs. Bedard led all students in a follow-up discussion about their scripts and performances. She also asked them to talk about some of the challenges they had. All of the students realized that their scripts needed work before they would be comprehensible to an audience, and they were eager to refine them. According to Mrs. Bedard:

> The students realized that they should have read the material more carefully. Some students said they focused too much on details and others said that the task made them realize that they didn't have the "big picture." They also discussed how they should have included a setting and introduction of characters to help situate the scene. All of the students wanted to do another Readers Theater, and they had good ideas about how they would do a better job next time.

Mrs. Bedard said she was pleased with the activity because it helped students with their writing and reading comprehension and because it gave them an opportunity to work collaboratively to accomplish a meaningful task:

> I think it helped the students spot weaknesses in their reading, and it provided an opportunity for them to discuss the book and think about how character dialogue can help the reader paint a picture of what a character is like. The students worked well together. Every student contributed I think because they all wanted a part. One student was initially unhappy with his part and the group revised the script and added more lines for him.

*During a social studies unit about westward expansion, Mrs. Bedard and her class read Karen Hesse's* Out of the Dust *(1997), a historical fiction novel about the Oklahoma dust bowl. In small groups, students wrote Readers Theater scripts based on different scenes from the novel. Mrs. Bedard guided students to craft their scripts so they would be understandable and interesting to the audience, and she gave them extra time and support to revise them. These boys are using the book as a resource as they discuss what to include in their script.*

## Brings Together Many Aspects of Literacy

In addition to fluency, Readers Theater addresses many other aspects of literacy, including reading, writing, listening, and thinking. Almost every state and literacy organization has developed standards for teaching language arts. The government has commissioned reports about best practices in literacy, and virtually every politician has an "education plan" with a major focus on literacy. All of these standards and reports include attention to several aspects of reading, including knowledge of the sounds of language, phonological awareness, decoding, word recognition, vocabulary, comprehension, and fluency. Teachers use a variety of approaches—reading aloud, guided reading, phonics instruction, independent reading, and direct instruction—to address these components. As I will discuss in the next section, Readers Theater is a comprehensive method that includes attention to all of these approaches and components. Teachers can therefore feel confident that, when they use Readers Theater, they will be attending to nationally accepted standards for literacy instruction.

## Can Be Used Across the Curriculum

Readers Theater is a fun, effective way to teach reading and content subjects, such as science, history, literature, and even mathematics. Wherever you use reading, research, and writing, you can use Readers Theater to focus or supplement your instruction. Box 1-2 on page 20 lists some of the possibilities for using Readers Theater across the curriculum.

## Reaches a Range of Students

In the intermediate grades—grades 3 through 6—individual differences among students become increasingly pronounced. Within a single classroom, students have a wide range of instructional strengths and challenges. Some may struggle with word identification and fluency, some with comprehension, others with writing. Even when their academic skills are fine, some students struggle with motivation and engagement or with social interaction skills.

The intermediate grades also bring special academic demands, particularly in content areas. As students move through the years, we expect them to read better, faster, and more independently. Even students who have previously done well in school may be frustrated by increasing reading demands. They may begin to doubt their academic abilities, question the value of schoolwork, and decrease their efforts in school.

If you're like many intermediate-grade teachers, you are probably wondering if Readers Theater will work for this full range of students you encounter regularly. You may be picturing specific students and thinking, "No way." Nothing has worked so far, so why should Readers Theater?

Studies of Readers Theater have found that it is beneficial for students with a variety of needs. For example, the resistant readers studied by Tyler and Chard (2000) enjoyed working with peers to prepare Readers Theater performances. They reread their scripts many times and eagerly engaged in practice for performances. Teachers and researchers who have examined the use of Readers Theater in tutorial settings have found that it gives students confidence and motivates them to read on their own (Rinehart, 1999; Worthy, Broaddus, & Ivey, 2001). Rinehart (1999) found that the students in a summer remedial reading program improved in word recognition, comprehension, oral reading, self-confidence, and motivation. He concluded, "These students were excited about reading their scripts because

## The Many Uses of Readers Theater

**Additional uses for Readers Theater in language arts:**

⊙ **To introduce or advertise books, series, or authors.** After hearing a performance, many students decide to read the books or explore the author's works on their own (place these works in the classroom library and watch them disappear).

⊙ **As a culminating activity for a book club or literature circle.** Students can write scripts based on their favorite scenes.

⊙ **In writing workshop.** Writing scripts can be a regular workshop topic.

**Uses for Readers Theater in content areas (mathematics, science, social studies):**

⊙ **As an introduction to new topics.** For example, a scene from Pam Muñoz Ryan's *Esperanza Rising* can be used to set the stage for a study of immigration. Mildred Taylor's *The Gold Cadillac* or Christopher Paul Curtis's *The Watsons Go to Birmingham* can provide an entrée to the study of civil rights and discrimination.

⊙ **As a motivating way for students to learn new information.** For example, scripts based on Elinor Pinczes's *100 Hundred Hungry Ants* or Pat Hutchins's *The Doorbell Rang* will provide students with an active way to learn about division using different multiples. Performing scripts based on Christopher Maynard's *Micro Monsters: Life Under the Microscope* or other science books can be more motivating than simply reading the books.

⊙ **As a form of presenting research.** Students can organize their findings into Readers Theater scripts as a culmination to a research unit in any content area.

they *could* and someone wanted to listen" (p. 87). All of these studies found that practice is essential for students to read their parts with fluency and confidence. Some of the students were reluctant to perform in front of a group at first, but all lost their fear when given opportunities to practice a script with a teacher, tutor, or friends in a safe atmosphere. Each success led to increased self-confidence and to motivation to repeat the success. Readers Theater can be used in any subject area, in any context imaginable (from remedial reading, to bilingual and ESL, to advanced classes), and with all kinds of students.

In the following sections, I describe some challenging students and some typical classroom situations in which Readers Theater has made a difference. Chances are you'll recognize at least a couple of them.

## Students Who Resist Reading

Students in the intermediate grades have many things on their minds other than reading and school. Peers become more important. Interests become more focused, and many students are participating in more extracurricular activities. Even if they can keep up with their schoolwork, many students don't find the time, energy, or motivation to read for pleasure, and a vicious cycle begins. If students don't read, reading becomes more difficult. If reading is more difficult, students don't want to read. You get the picture. Yet, these years are crucial for developing the independent literacy skills students will need in middle school, high school, and later life.

Readers Theater is a "shot in the arm" for those students who have become bored with reading and schoolwork or for those who have had challenges with learning to read. It also provides a successful, fun, engaging experience in which students can work productively with their peers toward a meaningful goal: presenting a performance.

## Students Who Are Learning English

Classroom teachers frequently remark that Readers Theater helps English language learners to improve their oral language fluency and motivation to read. Thuong, a fourth grader who had recently emigrated from Vietnam, was a skilled reader of Vietnamese, but was just beginning to read English. Her ESL teacher, Mr. Kelly, often used folk and fairy tales as English reading material because the students enjoyed them. They were also relatively easy to read and provided a familiar story structure for students who were learning English. He started using Readers Theater to give his students an incentive to read the stories multiple times.

Thuong, who loved being the center of attention, begged Mr. Kelly to let her play the starring role in Linda Williams's *The Little Old Lady Who Was Not Afraid of Anything* (1988) (see Appendix, page 97, for the script). Mr. Kelly was hesitant. There were many students who could easily read the central character's part and many parts that Thuong would be able to read more easily. Mr. Kelly did not want Thuong to be embarrassed, but he decided to go for it and give her the part. Thuong rose to the challenge, practicing her part at home and improving every day. In the performance, her reading *and* her acting were the hit of the show, and her English language and literacy continued to improve steadily.

Francisco, a fifth grader from Guatemala, had been in a bilingual education program since his arrival in the United States four years before. He had learned to speak, read, and write English fluently, but his mother was concerned that he was "losing his Spanish." Although her instruction was primarily in English, Francisco's teacher decided to include a "Spanish week," with all-Spanish scripts, in her Readers Theater unit. Francisco was in the group that performed *Estrellita de Oro* (Hayes, 2002), a Latino Cinderella story. On his first reading, Francisco stumbled through his part, embarrassed that, for once, his reading was not among the most fluent in the class. But after practicing all week with his teenage sister, Francisco read his part fluently and expressively at the performance, with his proud mother in attendance.

## Students Who Struggle With Reading

When my son was in third grade, I volunteered to help his teacher in the classroom. Since I was an experienced classroom teacher and reading specialist, she gave me the "low group." She warned me that the students in the group were not only struggling with reading, they had also developed a very negative attitude about it. In terms of behavior, she cautioned, "They'll give you a run for your money." She was right, but the materials she gave me to use with them were a large part of the problem. They were old basal readers with stories that bored me to tears, and the students could barely read a word in the books. Although I had worked with many struggling students, these kids were more hostile toward reading than any others I'd encountered, and they took it out on me. I couldn't blame them. I began dreading going to the school.

I was ready to give up but, instead, I asked the teacher if I could use some different materials. I chose a book that was fun to read and would provide some support for the students: Paul Galdone's version of *The Three Billy Goats Gruff* (1981). First I read it aloud and then I wrote a script and gave students their own copies. We started by reading all of the parts together until every student could read every part well. Then the students chose roles and took their scripts home to practice. The change in their attitudes was overwhelming as we practiced together. They knew they were reading well, and their motivation and confidence grew by leaps and bounds. We kept our work secret until we had a chance to perform for the class. The students read their parts fluently and played their roles perfectly, from the tiniest Billy Goat Gruff, who spoke in a high-pitched, nervous voice, to the Troll, who was "as mean as he was ugly." The teacher was nothing less than shocked, and the other students in the class begged to be allowed to do plays, too.

So how do I suggest you meet the needs of your challenged readers when you are teaching a whole class (not just the "low group" as I was in this situation)? To start, choose a script that is easy for the majority of students. Read the story aloud first (so they've heard a model of what it sounds like), and then read the script chorally several times. While students are reading their scripts independently, go around the room and coach, focusing on the challenged readers. Then let students take the scripts home to practice before they even rehearse with their group. (See Chapter 3 for a more complete description of an introductory lesson.)

## Students Who Are Shy About Reading

At one of my workshops, a fifth-grade teacher, Mrs. Berger, shared the story of Trinidad, a boy who she said was "afraid of his own shadow." He never talked in class. Even when Mrs. Berger asked him a direct question, he spoke softly and used as few words as possible. Not surprisingly, when the subject of Readers Theater came up, both Mrs. Berger and Trinidad assumed he wouldn't be participating. While the rest of the class worked in groups on performances, Trinidad read silently at his desk. After two weeks of watching his classmates perform, Trinidad took Mrs. Berger aside and told her, "I'll be in a play if you want me to." Mrs. Berger did the right thing by following Trinidad's lead. She didn't push, and she didn't make him feel badly for not participating. He made the choice when he was ready. Trinidad did not want to be a "star," as some students do. While other students fought over the juicier character roles, Trinidad always requested the part of the narrator. He was not interested in being the center of attention, but he did want to work with his classmates.

There are other approaches to helping quiet or timid students "work up" to performing. They might practice in private, with a friend, or with the teacher, and decide when they are ready to perform. They

> **Box 1-3**
>
> **Tips for Students Who Are Shy About Reading**
>
> **The student can:**
>
> ◉ tape-record his/her reading, listen, and evaluate it
>
> ◉ prepare to read to a younger student or make an audio book
>
> ◉ read with a trusted friend or with the teacher
>
> ◉ use a puppet
>
> ◉ perform the script as a radio play, in which the audience hears the voices but does not necessarily see the performers
>
> ◉ practice in a private place, "such as outside, or behind a screen, or under your desk" (Sebesta, 2003)

can share a part with a classmate or participate in reading a group part. The narrator's part can be a good bridge to parts that require more acting. The narrator can sit or stand to the side, out of sight if they wish. Another way to be somewhat anonymous is to wear a mask. (Be sure students' mouths are not covered). Often, the quietest students actually enjoy performing character parts once they get used to the idea. But it is important to realize that some students will never choose to participate in Readers Theater performances, and they should not be pressured as long as they are engaging in similar activities. Box 1-3 lists some of the most effective tips for working with shy readers.

## Students Who Say They Hate to Read

Because of my background in working with challenged and resistant learners, I am often called upon by teachers who are worried about a particular student in their classroom. These are typically students who not only resist reading but who actively claim to "*hate* reading." Although it sometimes takes weeks, the teacher and I usually have found the right combination of materials and appropriate instruction to reach even these most resistant readers . . . that is, until I met Jenny. I have never known a student who hated reading more than Jenny.

*A little moral support can go a long way for a student who is shy or reluctant to perform in front of a group. This fourth grader and his teacher read a Shel Silverstein poem together.*

A fifth grader, Jenny was a nice girl who would at least try to do almost anything she was assigned in school, but she was clearly not interested in school tasks. According to her teacher, Mrs. Howard, she *never* chose to read on her own. Her lack of reading practice showed. She was more than two years behind grade level, and would be off to middle school in the fall. The future looked dim. Despite her teacher's caring attitude, skillful instruction, vast classroom library, and very large bag of tricks, Jenny remained apathetic toward school tasks. Reading was at the top of her "not-to-do" list.

During the spring, Mrs. Howard started a unit on Readers Theater. She predicted that Jenny would not want to participate, not only because she did not like to read, but because she rarely spoke in class. Fortunately, Mrs. Howard was wrong. The first set of scripts she used was based on Marc Brown's Arthur series (e.g., *Arthur's Birthday*, 1991). As Mrs. Howard had predicted, Jenny at first refused to participate. The second week, she chose the part with the fewest lines (two). At the beginning of the third week, to Mrs. Howard's surprise, Jenny announced that she wanted to play the part of Arthur's little sister DW, the part with the most lines. Even more surprising, at that week's performance, Jenny "became" DW, reading her part with no mistakes and with expression. "I practiced with my cousin," Jenny explained to her shocked classmates and teacher. Readers Theater made an amazing difference in Jenny's motivation to read on her own, in her comfort level in the classroom and, ultimately, in her reading ability. Mrs. Howard noticed a tremendous difference in her other students' reading motivation as well. She shared, "After every Readers Theater performance, the first words I hear are 'Can I read [the book]?' I have had students actually fighting over books, so I had to start a sign-up sheet." Mrs. Howard's only regret was that she had not begun using Readers Theater sooner.

Time after time, teachers have told me about previously reluctant readers who practiced at home, sometimes with their families, and came alive during their Readers Theater performances. For example, I once heard about a group that was in a panic one Friday because the student who had both starring roles in Harry Allard's *Miss Nelson is Missing* (1985) (she was both Miss Nelson and Viola Swamp) was absent from school. Another student, Isabel, who was known for her passionate dislike of reading, told them not to worry. She had practiced all week at home and knew every part. She stepped in and saved the show. And Isabel's case is not an isolated one: "Most teachers find that even the most resistant readers practice their Readers Theater scripts as if they were doing a full-time job—and one that they love" (Prescott, 2003).

# Final Thought

You probably wouldn't be reading this book if you weren't positively inclined to use innovative approaches like Readers Theater in your classroom. At this point, however, you may be thinking that your day is already too full to add something that may seem mostly like enrichment (even with the promises I've made in this chapter). The school curriculum is already full of constraints and accountability, and many teachers have to justify everything they do as being "research based." And these days, in addition to being expected to cover all aspects of language arts, teachers are getting a particularly strong message about helping their students develop reading fluency.

This final point, however, may be just what you need to convince yourself, colleagues, or administrators that Readers Theater is well worth the time and effort. In the next chapter, I will discuss the research foundations of Readers Theater that relate specifically to fluent reading. In Reader Theater, students read texts repeatedly to practice for performances. Thus, as in conventional methods of fluency instruction, Readers Theater improves students' rate of reading and accuracy.  As you will see, though, fluent reading is not just a matter of reading quickly and accurately but also of reading smoothly and with appropriate expression. Because students must interpret as well as read accurately and quickly, Readers Theater helps them take their fluency to a higher level in ways that traditional methods of fluency instruction cannot.

# Chapter 2

# Readers Theater Develops Fluency

**M**eet Joshua Darby, a good student who has always done his homework and brought home As and Bs. Or at least he did until this year. Now that Josh is in fourth grade, school is getting tougher, and he is starting to fall behind. His mother says he spends so much time on his homework that he hardly has time to play with his friends or read his beloved comic books. He complains every day about going to school and now says he hates to read. Josh's teacher says he still loves it when she reads aloud to the class, but he is starting to goof off during content-area instruction and at other times when he has to read himself. He is often one of the last students to finish reading, and sometimes his follow-up assignments show a fuzzy understanding of the material. It's not that Josh can't figure out the words and comprehend fourth-grade books. The problem is that it takes so long because Josh is not a fluent reader. His reading is slow and choppy, and he has to spend a lot of effort to figure out words and make sense of what he reads.

What Josh is experiencing is common in the intermediate grades, when the reading load gets heavier and more difficult, and students are expected to do more work independently. For students who are not fluent readers, these demands are sometimes too much; they lose self-confidence and the motivation to read, so they don't read much. And because they don't read much, their reading doesn't improve and they fall farther and farther behind. Students like Josh need to improve their fluency so they will be able to keep up with schoolwork and also so they won't become resistant to reading. That's where Readers Theater comes in. In this chapter, I review research about fluency, describe traditional approaches to fluency instruction, and explain why Readers Theater is a better alternative.

# What Is Reading Fluency and Why Is It Important?

Fluency gives language its musical quality, its rhythm and flow. Think of a newscaster announcing a late-breaking news story or a spokesperson on a commercial. They can talk you into tuning in to the news or buying the newest luxury. It's hard not to be affected by a voice like that of poet Maya Angelou; actors James Edward Olmos, Meryl Streep, and Anthony Hopkins; activists such as Martin Luther King and César Chavez; or politicians such as John F. Kennedy or Ronald Reagan. Effective public speakers are not just polished and poised; when they speak, they draw us in and hold our attention.

Fluent reading sounds like fluent speaking—effortless, smooth, and graceful. But fluent reading is not as easy as it sounds, especially for young readers. Even for expert readers, reading a story out loud to a group takes thought and practice. A fluent reader must be able to decode and recognize words automatically and read accurately, quickly, and smoothly, with the right intonation and with expression. Being able to read a text with fluency is about more than sounding good; it's about understanding and interpreting the text. In a world that is increasingly dependent on reading and understanding large quantities of information in our homes, schools, and workplaces, fluency is an essential aspect of reading.

# How Fluent Reading Develops

Fluent reading is built on many experiences with reading, listening, and speaking. Even before they begin school, children should have many experiences with print and oral language. They should listen to stories and informational texts, and they should have opportunities to talk about and explore books. Children who have had these kinds of supportive experiences will enter school with an understanding of the functions of reading, as well as positive feelings about learning to read. An effective early literacy program will build upon students' home language and literacy experiences and provide additional experiences for children who have had limited experience.

Fluency continues to develop as teachers read aloud with expression and share their enthusiasm for reading. A classroom that fosters fluent reading development is full of interesting, well-written materials on every topic imaginable. In such a classroom, students have many opportunities to explore, read, and share reading materials with others. It can take many years and many successful reading experiences for reading fluency to develop.

However, if reading experiences are pleasurable and meaningful and access to books is plentiful, children are more likely to engage in reading. And engagement is one of the most important building blocks of fluency (Elley, 2000; Ivey & Broaddus, 2001; Neuman, 1999).

Fluency also depends on reading words accurately, so proficient decoding skills are essential (Adams, 1990). Students need practice to recognize words quickly and automatically, reading with appropriate phrasing rather than word by word. They need many experiences reading in texts that provide just the right amount of challenge and support so they can develop confidence and a "feel" for smooth reading. Simply put, to develop fluency, students need to read a lot. As automatic reading develops, the reader is able to focus attention primarily on meaning rather than on features of print (Samuels, 1994). True fluency—reading with appropriate timing, expressiveness, stress, and intonation—depends on being able to understand and interpret text (Dowhower, 1991; Strecker, Roser, & Martinez, 1999).

*These boys find a quiet place outside of the classroom to get in some extra rehearsal time for an upcoming Readers Theater performance.*

Some students seem to easily develop fluency if they have heard good reading models and had plenty of experience with reading. However, many need instruction that targets fluency development. All students, including skilled readers, will benefit from such instruction. (See Timothy Rasinski's book, *The Fluent Reader: Oral Reading Strategies for Building Word Recognition, Fluency, and Comprehension*, 2003, for a more thorough discussion.) The next section briefly describes the most common form of fluency instruction: repeated reading.

# Repeated Reading

In the past few years, educators have been told that they should use "research-based reading practices." It is indeed essential that instructional practices be based on sound theory and research. Repeated reading, a tested and proven method for increasing reading fluency in short term studies, certainly meets this criterion. (See review in the National Reading Panel report, 2000.) Reading researchers have found that repeated reading is an effective way of improving word recognition, speed, and phrasal reading, and that the benefits can transfer to new texts.

Repeated reading is just what it sounds like. The idea is that if something is read repeatedly, fluency will improve. There are several variations on repeated reading. For example, repeated reading is a major focus of shared reading (Holdaway, 1979), a common practice in primary classrooms. Students listen to and attempt to make their reading sound like an expert reader through reading along with the teacher (choral reading) or by repeating what the teacher has read (echo reading). Books on tape can also be used as models of fluent reading and for independent practice in repeated reading (Chomsky, 1978; Worthy, Broaddus, & Ivey, 2001).

Readers Theater is another way of engaging students in repeated reading. In Readers Theater, students read their parts many times as they practice for performances. However, there are some key differences between straightforward repeated reading and the Readers Theater version of this technique. In my opinion and experience, Readers Theater is far more effective at addressing the areas of reading fluency, comprehension, and motivation. I examine why in more detail below.

# The Problems With Using Repeated Reading Alone

So why bother with Readers Theater? Why not just use repeated reading and be done with it? As every teacher knows, teaching methods that are effective in research settings don't always transfer perfectly to the classroom. There are a number of reasons why repeated reading by itself is not the ideal classroom method. Below are a few.

## STUDENTS COMPLAIN, "WE ALREADY READ IT!"

While very young children love to hear and read the same books over and over, the story is usually very different with older students. Ask your students to reread a book and you will likely hear, "But I already read it." Imagine how you would feel if someone told you that you would have to read the same book or passage again and again if you wanted to improve your reading. While research has shown repeated reading to be effective in the short run, it does not typically hold students' attention over long periods. One way around this conundrum is to start with a text that students can read and understand. The teacher may read the text aloud first and discuss it with students; more advanced readers may be able to read the text independently. Have students reread the text until they reach an appropriate level of speed and accuracy. Give them a stopwatch and show them how to time their readings and graph their progress. Although this is initially fun and motivating for some students, the novelty usually wears off quickly.

*These students are practicing their Readers Theater scripts for an upcoming performance. They are completely engaged and on task, reading and rereading as they simultaneously focus on expression and character interpretation.*

# PRACTICE WITHOUT PERFORMANCE CAN WEAR THIN

Repeated reading by itself can be like continually practicing without ever playing a game. Anyone who has tried to convince students to read by telling them that "practice makes perfect" knows that this isn't the ideal method. Imploring (or nagging) students to practice gets old fast. What do you find more interesting and motivating: Practicing musical scales or playing a duet with your friend? Doing passing drills or scrimmaging? I don't mean to imply that practice isn't important, because of course it is. However, doing something meaningful is always more fun—and usually more effective—than simply practicing.

# REPEATED READING DOES NOT SPECIFICALLY ADDRESS COMPREHENSION AND INTERPRETATION

The most serious problem with repeated reading is its unilateral focus on accuracy and speed. Just as it is possible to play a musical piece with technical accuracy but limited feeling and flow, it is possible to read with accuracy, speed, and appropriate phrasing but without understanding (Aaron, 1989; Worthy & Invernizzi, 1996). Although it is important that students comprehend the texts used for repeated reading, this method does not specifically address comprehension and interpretation.

With a focus only on accuracy and speed, students can get the badly mistaken impression that reading is mainly about sounding good and reading quickly rather than understanding what one reads. When you think about it, reading a text repeatedly just to increase speed is almost like taking only aspirin for an infection. The symptoms of pain and fever (slow reading) might lessen or even disappear for a while. However, the infection or root of the problem (reading for meaning) is still there and is only masked by the treatment. For example, students may be able to decode the words in a science textbook or "read" a foreign language with ease if they know how

*Reading comprehension and fluency are both critical elements of preparing for and performing a successful Readers Theater production.*

the language works. But if they don't understand and cannot interpret what they're reading, they are not reading with genuine fluency no matter how smooth they sound. To demonstrate what I mean to preservice and inservice teachers, I often use the following paragraph from a book called *Synopsis of Neuroanatomy* (Matzke & Foltz, 1983):

> A poorly myelinated or nonmyelinated fiber branches profusely and ends as a naked terminal among the epithelial cells of the skin and viscera, in subcutaneous tissue, and in the walls of blood vessels. These naked nerve endings are the nociceptors, but many are also polymodal in that they may respond to thermal and mechanical stimulation. Some fibers terminate in a cup-like expansion in relation to a specialized epithelial cell. (p. 28)

I have practiced this passage several times (using repeated reading) and can read it smoothly, rapidly, and accurately. Yet, if someone asked me to explain it, I wouldn't have the slightest idea of what to say. I have no idea what it means, and I realize that. The first stanza from Lewis Carroll's nonsense poem, *Jabberwocky,* illustrates the same idea:

> 'Twas brillig, and the slithy toves
> Did gyre and gimble in the wade;
> All mimsy were the borogoves,
> And the mome raths outgrabe.

The syntax allows you to read it with expression and appropriate phrasing, even though the major words in the poem are made up. Clearly, it is not enough just to read quickly and accurately and to *sound* fluent. If I were a student learning to read and people told me that I was a "good reader" simply because I could form the words quickly and even phrase them correctly, I might not work so hard to understand what I'm reading. We have all worked with this kind of student. They sound fine, but they don't "get it." Reading without comprehension is not reading. Likewise, comprehension is a nonnegotiable aspect of genuine fluency.

*These students from Mrs. Bedard's language arts class regularly adapt novels for Readers Theater and perform for their classmates and other audiences.*

# Why Readers Theater Is a Better Choice for Improving Fluency

Readers Theater addresses the pitfalls of repeated reading and still provides the benefits. It provides students with an authentic reason to engage in repeated reading of texts (Rhinehart, 1999; Tyler and Chard, 2000; Worthy, Broaddus, & Ivey, 2001). Readers Theater is an inherently meaningful, purposeful vehicle for repeated reading. It is something that students actually *want* to do.

To get ready for Readers Theater performances, students want to practice because they know that their practice will ultimately lead to a performance, and they want to make *sure* that they do their very best. Thus, practice becomes a meaningful means to an end, and you can accomplish the same goals as repeated reading (and more) without nagging students to practice. As one third grader said, "I practiced hard so I wouldn't mess up."

Lois Walker, who taught college drama and produced theater and children's television for many years and who has published many children's scripts, is one of Readers Theater's greatest fans and promoters. As she puts it:

> Think about it: if you agreed to read aloud in front of a group, wouldn't *YOU* be sure you knew how to pronounce the words and understood what they meant? You might even rehearse a bit at home before the reading.

No kidding. Can you think of anything more important to your students than peer pressure? Why not use it positively?

In addition, Readers Theater encourages students to read at an appropriate rate rather than to simply read faster without regard to the text's meaning. In fact, Readers Theater not only specifically addresses comprehension, it *enhances* it. A student's ability to perform a part in a play does more than make her sound like a good reader; it is evidence that she comprehends what she is reading. When students narrate a text or play the part of a character, they not only have to "get it," they are also responsible for presenting the text in a way that makes their audience get it. So rather than simply working to improve speed and accuracy, with Readers Theater students need to "dig in" and comprehend their part deeply and thoroughly. When they read and interpret texts regularly and listen to others' reading and interpretations, they make progress in all aspects of reading.

# Final Thought

Now you've heard *why* Readers Theater is a great instructional approach. Not only can your students practice fluency without getting bored, with Readers Theater they are simultaneously reading and interpreting good books. And a bonus I've found is that students don't fool around much with Readers Theater. They take it seriously because they really like it, and they know they will be performing for an audience rather than for a stopwatch or a tape recorder.

In the next chapter, in order to help you learn *how* to implement Readers Theater in your classroom, I offer organizational tips and lessons that are appropriate for all elementary grades. Because every classroom is different, I'll also share with you some ways that different teachers have made Readers Theater work for them.

# Chapter 3

# Getting Organized and Setting the Stage

There's an unwritten law in teaching that it can take weeks to establish a "well-oiled" classroom community that will run smoothly for the school year. Students and teachers need time to get to know one another. Students need explicit directions and guidelines—along with modeling, demonstration, and practice—to learn the classroom rules, procedures, and routines. This initial investment will help ensure a more efficient classroom community where everyone can get along and make the most of instructional time.

After this initial community is established, experienced teachers find that each time a new instructional approach is introduced, a similar albeit much shorter period of adjustment—complete with modeling, demonstration, and practice—is needed. This chapter addresses the introduction period for Readers Theater.

In this chapter, I first share some basic guidelines and tips for gathering, organizing, and storing scripts and other supplies. (See Box 3-1 for a checklist.) Then, I address how to introduce Readers Theater to students. I include three lesson plans to help you provide students with an overview of Readers Theater basics, along with some guided practice in fluent reading and interpretation. Finally, I offer some possible schedules and routines for implementing Readers Theater and some variations suggested by teachers.

# Supplies

Three ingredients are essential to successful Readers Theater: scripts, costumes, and props. In this section, I offer advice on gathering and organizing those supplies.

## SCRIPTS

One of the greatest benefits of Readers Theater is that is does not require special, expensive materials as traditional plays often do. Rather than using elaborate scenery and costumes, in Readers Theater performances, the story is conveyed mainly through readers' voices and facial expressions. The most important supplies for Readers Theater are copies of scripts for rehearsals and performances. For more detailed information on finding and creating scripts, see Chapter 4. Once you've chosen or created a script:

- Provide multiple copies of each as "rehearsal scripts." Students will use these for reading, practicing, rehearsing, and making notes for performances.

- Create a set of "performance scripts" which are always kept in the classroom and are used only during performances. This ensures that there will be copies for performance day even if students lose or forget

> **Three Readers Theater Scripts**
> **Based on the Book *Fox at School***
> **by Edward Marshall**
>
> ## 1. "Fox in Charge"
>
> | CAST | Narrator | Carmen | Dexter | Fox |
> | --- | --- | --- | --- | --- |
> | | Miss Moon | Principal | Class (3 or 4 students) | |
>
> **Narrator:** [*Shows the book and introduces the characters.*] The title of this book is *Fox at School*, and it's written by Edward Marshall. The book has three stories about Fox and his friends. This story is called "Fox in Charge."
> **Narrator:** Carmen, Dexter, and Fox were on their way to school.
> **Carmen:** I'm going to be a pilot when I grow up.
> **Dexter:** I think I'll be a cowboy.
> **Carmen:** What about you, Fox?
> **Fox:** I'm going to be a teacher.
> **Carmen:** You're not serious.
> **Fox:** It's an easy job.
> **Narrator:** The next morning Fox was in for a big surprise.
> **Miss Moon:** I must be away for a few minutes, and I'm putting Fox in charge.
> **Fox:** Hot dog!
> **Miss Moon:** Keep them under control.
> **Fox:** Don't worry about a thing.
> **Miss Moon:** You will mind Fox.
> **Class:** Yes, Miss Moon.
> **Miss Moon:** I'll be back.
>
> *Readers Theater for Building Fluency • Scholastic Teaching Resources*　　85

*Use different-colored highlighters to mark roles on Readers Theater scripts, so students can find their parts easily and won't lose their places during performances.*

their own copies. Each set of scripts should include a highlighted copy for each role. Lois Walker (2003) suggests:

If possible, place cast scripts in colorful folders. Ring binders allow for smooth and easy page turning. If ring binders are not available, staple cast scripts along left-hand side into simple cardboard folders. Crease the pages about a half an inch inside the staples for easy page turning.

◉ Make available the book upon which the script is based. When students are rehearsing, they will use the book as a resource for planning performances. When performances are introduced, the students will show the book to the audience. These books should stay in the classroom. If possible, keep a copy of the book in the classroom library as well. (Remember, students always like to read books that have been performed in Readers Theater.) If you have only one copy of the book, be sure it is returned to the Readers Theater center each day. (See Box 3-1.)

## COSTUMES AND PROPS

While you should choose (or write) scripts that convey information through words and not objects, simple costumes and props can help performers get into character and aid in audience understanding and enjoyment (Wolf, 1993). Important rules of thumb for costumes and props are (a) keep them simple so they don't distract the audience or performers, (b) be sure that they don't interfere with the performer's ability to perform or read the script, (c) let the script guide the kinds of extras you use.

*Write character names on strips of tag board and have students wear them as headbands, or use yarn to hang nametags around performers' necks.*

Students are generally able and happy to make costumes and props at home, so there might not even be a need to use class time for this.

## Costumes

Performers usually only need to wear simple character nametags made of tag board rather than costumes. Students can decide if they need additional items to enhance their characters, such as hats, glasses, and animals ears. For example, in the story "Fox on Stage" (see Appendix, page 88, for the script) Fox can wear sunglasses and a crown made of tag board or construction paper. In *How to Eat Fried Worms* (Rockwell, 1973) (see Appendix, page 106, for the script), the characters can wear items that signal they are active boys, like baseball caps and bandages. If one student plays two parts, costumes can help the audience to distinguish between the two characters. For example, when performing a script of *Miss Nelson is Missing* (Allard, 1977), the change from Miss Nelson to Viola Swamp could be signaled with a simple dark wig (made of yarn, black opaque pantyhose, or butcher paper).

*This student's mask leaves his mouth uncovered so the audience can hear his voice. It is attached with yarn, thereby leaving his hands free to hold the script.*

Simple masks can add interest and help a shy student feel less nervous about performing in front of an audience. Be sure masks do not cover students' mouths and do not interfere with their ability to hold scripts.

Bobbi Salinas's *Los Tres Cerdos/The Three Little Pigs* (1998) (see Appendix, page 82, for the script) gives easy directions to make a braided wig for Mamá Pig from a pair of black pantyhose. Ears and noses for the pigs and wolf are made from paper cups and construction paper, and held in place with yarn.

## Props

A few props can add visual appeal and help convey important story details. Always be on the lookout to collect items that students might use to enhance their performances (see Box 3-1). For example, in the story "Fox Escapes" in Edward Marshall's *Fox at School* (1983) (see Appendix, page 87, for the script), it would be helpful to have a bell to use for the fire drill. A typewriter would be an important prop for performing the story *Click, Clack, Moo: Cows That Type* by Doreen Cronin (2000), though an old computer keyboard could be a stand-in. (Most schools have them hidden away somewhere.) Chairs and bowls would add interest to a performance of "Goldilocks and the Three Bears."

*Keep a variety of props on hand—including items like hats, telephones, keyboards, coffee cups, watering cans, and glasses—for students to use in performances.*

## ORGANIZING SUPPLIES

Organization is a key to Readers Theater. Designate a Readers Theater center in your room or set aside a cabinet or bookshelf for your supplies. Include scripts and items for simple props and costumes. (See Box 3-1 for a checklist of materials.) Also, include space for a bulletin board or charts with reminders and announcements. Keeping all of your materials together and easily accessible makes things go more smoothly and helps to avoid "surprises," such as lost scripts and missing props.

> **Box 3-1**
>
> ### Readers Theater Supplies Checklist
>
> ____ Scripts for rehearsals and performances
>
> ____ Books on which the scripts are based
>
> ____ Tagboard and yarn for making character name tags and signs
>
> ____ Box of costume extras including fake mustaches, animal noses, old hats and glasses, and other accessories. Also include old bed sheets, butcher paper, yarn, and construction paper for making wigs and simple clothing.
>
> ____ Box of props including kitchen items, old electronic equipment, and other discarded objects

# Getting Started: Lessons to Introduce Readers Theater

For Readers Theater to be successful, students need a teacher-guided introduction. This section contains three lesson plans to help you provide students with an overview of Readers Theater basics, along with some guided practice in fluent reading and interpretation. After the lesson plans, I offer some possible schedules for implementing Readers Theater and some variations suggested by teachers.

For all kinds of instructional activities, researchers and educators recommend a "gradual release of responsibility" model, in which students gradually assume increased responsibility for their own learning (Graves, Juel, & Graves, 2004; Pearson & Gallagher, 1983). The lesson plans in this chapter follow this time-tested, research-based approach to learning. They are meant to be used consecutively at the beginning of the year or whenever you start Readers Theater. Start by doing most of the work yourself—by demonstrating, explaining, and modeling. Then give students an opportunity to try out the new activity with a high degree of support from you. Gradually release responsibility for learning to your students as you guide their practice, observe their progress, and decide when they are ready to move toward more independent work.

The first lesson here is in two parts, and introduces the whys, whats, and hows of Readers Theater. It also provides teacher-led practice. The lesson should take a total of 35 to 45 minutes, depending on the amount of support needed by students. Lesson Two, which should take about 30 minutes, is optional and provides a review and additional supported practice. In Lesson Three, also about 30 minutes, students practice independently and in groups with less support. After these initial lessons, students will be ready to work more independently (with you giving them support as needed) to practice and perform Readers Theater.

## INTRODUCTION LESSON

I like to introduce Readers Theater with one script for the entire class that is readable by virtually all of my students. One of my favorites is an adaptation of *The Boy Who Cried Wolf*, a fairy tale retold by Freya Littledale (1987) (see Appendix, page 79, for the script). In this story, a bored shepherd boy decides to get some attention by playing a trick on the people of his town.

Although the script may look very simple for intermediate-grade students, there are several important reasons to start with it or a similar text. The plot and characters' motives are straightforward. The story is short, easy to read, and simple yet dramatic—qualities that provide students the opportunity to focus on character interpretation and reading with appropriate expression. The script has three group parts (the fisherman, the townspeople, and the hunters) that can be shared by students who have reading challenges, who are shy, or who are reluctant to participate. Even confident readers have fun with the parts, and struggling readers will be able to participate without anxiety about reading the words, especially after they have heard the text read aloud. Following is a model lesson demonstrating how I would introduce Readers Theater.

GOALS: To introduce students to the basics of Readers Theater and explain its benefits (improving reading fluency and skill, understanding and interpreting literature).

CONTENT: In the first part of the lesson, the teacher introduces Readers Theater and explains the goals for the approach. The teacher reads aloud the book on which the script is based, models how to read dialogue with appropriate voice and facial expression, and gives students guided practice and feedback as they work with lines from the script. In Part II, students learn how a Readers Theater script is organized and practice reading the script independently and with the class.

MATERIALS:
  ⊙ The book *The Boy Who Cried Wolf* by Freya Littledale (Scholastic)
  ⊙ Copies of the script for every student in your class or group (See Appendix, page 79)
  ⊙ Sentence strips with lines from the script

## Preparation

Practice reading aloud *The Boy Who Cried Wolf* (Littledale, 1987) just as you would read any story to the class. Choose eight to ten lines or passages from the script and write them on sentence strips (see box for suggested lines). Include a line from all or most of the roles to help demonstrate a range of oral and facial expressions. Include several lines for main characters. I selected Tom's lines to demonstrate the range of his emotions as he moves through being bored, pretending to be scared, experiencing real fear when the wolf actually appears, and feeling frustration that the other characters don't believe him when he truly needs their help.

It is also important to include one or more narrator lines. Some students will not want to play the role of the narrator since it is seems less exciting than character roles. However, if you demonstrate the narrator's role and show how the subtle nuances of voice and facial expression can help the audience understand the story, students will usually be more willing to play that part.

| | |
|---|---|
| **Tom:** | Nothing ever happens to me. I see hunters hunting in the woods and fisherman fishing in the lake. But I just sit here and watch my sheep. |
| **Narrator 1:** | And so he did. He watched the sheep eat the grass. He watched them sleep in the sun. He watched them follow the leader along the side of the hill. |
| **Tom:** | Help! Help! Help! A wolf is going to eat my sheep. |
| **Narrator 2:** | And he led the hunters down to the lake . . . and all around it. |
| **Hunters:** | Where's the wolf? |
| **Fishermen:** | Don't worry. We'll help you. |
| **Townspeople:** | We heard all about you. And you can't fool anyone here! |
| **Wolf:** | I like your sheep. I think I'll eat them for lunch. |
| **Tom:** | But I'm not fooling this time. I'm telling the truth. Follow me and you'll see. |
| **Wolf:** | Heh! Heh! Heh! You told so many lies no one believed you when you told the truth! |

*continued . . .*

# PART I:
## Introducing Readers Theater and Practicing Interpretive Reading
### Teaching the Lesson

1. Introduce Readers Theater. Start by asking students if they have ever been in a play and what that was like. Explain how Readers Theater compares to other kinds of plays. You might say:

   In Readers Theater, the actors read their parts instead of memorizing them like they would in a regular play. Readers Theater scripts, like this one (show the script) are based on books that we have in our school. This script is based on *The Boy Who Cried Wolf* by Freya Littledale. We're going to be practicing and presenting our Readers Theaters to each other, and later we'll invite other classes and your families to be our audience.

2. Explain how Readers Theater helps students to become better, more fluent readers. You might say:

   Readers Theater is a fun thing to do, but it also helps us to read more fluently. Fluent reading means you can read smoothly, without many mistakes, and you can understand what you read. In Readers Theater, we become more fluent by reading the scripts many times. From reading the book and thinking and talking about the characters, we learn what makes them tick. This is called interpretation, and it helps us to read our lines so that we sound just like the character would sound and act just like the character would act, and so the audience doesn't get bored.

3. Read the book aloud, using appropriate expression. As you read, activate students' prior knowledge, ask them to predict the events, encourage them to make connections to their own lives, and talk with them about the characters. For example, you might ask students whether they have ever felt like Tom (bored and wanting attention) and what they did to get attention. Then ask them to predict what Tom will do next in the story and why they think what they do (e.g., "What have you learned about Tom that makes you think he might do that?"). Also ask students to predict the actions of the fishermen, hunters, and townspeople (e.g., "What do you think the fishermen will say to Tom now? Why do you think that?").

4. Show students the script version of the book and point out the various parts, including the characters and the narrator ("the person who tells the story"). Show the sentence strips one at a time (see box on page 38 for examples), and ask students to put themselves in the character's place as they read. The discussion might go something like this:

   Okay, pretend you are Tom watching your sheep at the beginning of the story. How are you feeling? Listen as I read the first line aloud, and think about how you would say it and what kind of expression you would have on your face: "Nothing ever happens to me. I see hunters hunting in the woods and fishermen fishing in the lake. But I just sit here and watch my sheep."

*continued . . .*

Call on a few students to give their interpretations of Tom's lines. When you discuss the narrator's lines, explain to students that, although the narrator is not a character, the role is very important in helping the audience understand the story. Go through the other lines in a similar way, modeling and coaching students to talk and act like the character (or narrator).

5. Provide additional practice in pairs. Let students work with the sentence strips in pairs. Encourage reading with appropriate expression; model and provide support as needed.

# PART II:
## Showing How a Readers Theater Script Is Organized, and Practicing in Small Groups
### Teaching the Lesson

1. Give each student a copy of the script and point out features such as the actors'/ characters' names and the dialogue ("the part that the characters say"). Give students a few minutes to read the script independently while you walk around and help them with unfamiliar words.

2. Have the class read the entire script chorally. Coach students to use appropriate expression (e.g., "Let's try that line again. If you were the Wolf, how would you say that?").

3. Assign roles. Choose volunteers for the individual parts (Narrators 1 and 2, Tom, Wolf). Assign the remaining parts to groups of students so that everyone has a part. Give students a few minutes to read through their parts independently and then reconvene to read through the script again.

4. Now that you've practiced the script several times, everyone should be familiar with all of the lines. Give students some time to practice more so that everyone has a chance to read through the entire script. (Depending upon your schedule, they can practice at home, in class the same day, or the next day).

5. Break the class into two groups, assign parts, and give students ten minutes to practice. Then have the groups present the play to each other.

## REVIEW LESSON

If you find that some students are struggling with the reading, need more practice, or are reluctant to participate, this optional lesson provides additional supported practice before moving on to small group work (Lesson Three). Lesson Two can be done with the whole class or with a small group, depending upon the needs of your students. It uses a story from *Fox at School*, a book in the popular Fox collection by Edward Marshall. The Fox books are great for Readers Theater because they feature a funny and clever character who is interesting enough to engage intermediate-level students, yet the books are easy to read. As students read more stories about Fox, they will gain insights into his character, and some students will choose to read other books in the series independently. The stories are also short, making them wonderful for multiple performances when time is an issue. Finally, scripts based on Fox books are easy for teachers and for students to write.

40

In this story selected for Lesson Two, Fox's teacher leaves the class for a few minutes and puts Fox in charge of his classmates. Fox, who has an overabundance of self-confidence, has no doubt that the students will do as he says. He soon finds out he's wrong. As soon as the teacher leaves, the classroom erupts into chaos. Being left in charge is something students will be able to identify with. Some students will have had experiences like Fox's, where they have felt out of control (or perhaps *they* will have been the troublemaker), so they will be able to identify with the characters and imagine how they will act and speak. Here's how I would structure this review lesson.

## LESSON TWO

# Reviewing Basic Procedures and Providing Additional Practice

**GOALS:** To review and extend students' understanding of the basic procedures and reasons behind Readers Theater and to give them additional supported practice in interpreting characters through voice and facial expressions.

**CONTENT:** The teacher reads aloud the book on which the script is based, modeling how to read expressively, and gives student guided practice and feedback in reading with appropriate expression. Students practice reading a script independently and with the group or class.

**MATERIALS:**
- ⊙ The book *Fox at School* by Edward Marshall (Puffin)
- ⊙ Copies of the script "Fox in Charge" for every student in your class or group (See Appendix, page 85)
- ⊙ Sentence strips with lines from the script

## Preparation

Practice reading aloud "Fox in Charge" from Marshall's *Fox at School* (1983) as you would read any story to the class. Read through the script. Choose eight to ten lines or passages from the script, sampling from most of the characters, and write them on sentence strips (see box for recommended lines).

| |
|---|
| **Narrator:** The next morning Fox was in for a big surprise. |
| **Moon:** You *will* mind Fox. |
| **Fox:** Don't worry about a thing. |
| **Class:** You can't make us. |
| **Fox:** I'm in charge here. You will do as I say. |
| **Class:** That's what you think! We're going to have some fun! |
| **Dexter:** You tricked us! Now we're really going to go hog-wild. |
| **Principal:** What is the meaning of this? |
| **Fox:** *Uh oh.* |

*continued . . .*

## Teaching the Lesson

1. Review what Readers Theater is and how it helps students to become better readers. (See page 39 for details.)

2. Read the story from the book using appropriate expression, asking students to predict the events and explain their predictions.

3. Model and let students practice character interpretation, using the lines written on sentence strips.

4. Hand out scripts and give students a few minutes to read them independently, helping them with difficult words.

5. Have the class or group read the entire script chorally, providing coaching as they go (e.g., "What is Carmen like?"; "If you were Carmen, how would you say that line?").

6. Assign each role to a student or group of students.

7. Give students a few minutes to read through their parts independently before presenting the play.

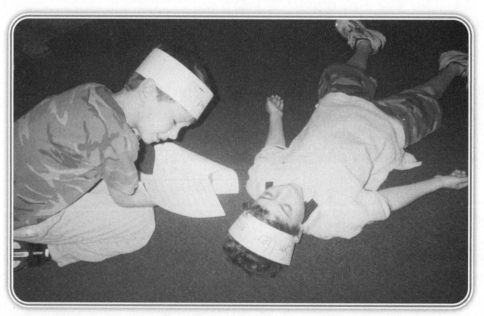

*In addition to practicing lines, performers need to decide how characters will act. Even non-speaking parts call for interpretation.*

## TRANSITION LESSON

Lesson Three is an intermediate step between the teacher-directed practice of the first two lessons and the more student-directed work of practicing and performing Readers Theater in small groups, which is described later in this chapter.

For this lesson, use the second story and script from *Fox at School*, "Fox Escapes" (see Appendix, page 87). In the story, the class participates in a fire drill in which they go down a slide from the second story window to the ground. The teacher, Miss Moon, starts out being

42

in charge, directing students to move quickly. However, when her turn on the slide comes, her fear makes her behave like a child. Although the story events and pictures show Miss Moon's feelings, her words do not. When Fox asks if she's afraid, she says, "Not on your life. *I always take the stairs.*"

In this lesson, you will direct students to use their voices, facial expressions, and actions to show the true feelings of Miss Moon and the other characters. At the end of the lesson, you will lead the class in a debriefing session to evaluate their interpretations. In later lessons, when students work in small groups to practice and perform different stories, they will be expected to do this type of interpretation without as much teacher support because you will be working with multiple groups and stories at the same time.

## LESSON THREE

# Offering Guided Practice in Small Groups

**GOALS:** To review Readers Theater procedures and to provide students with guided practice in rehearsing and performing a script as they move toward more student-directed work in Readers Theater.

**CONTENT:** The teacher reads and leads a discussion of a story from *Fox at School*. Then students practice and perform the script in two groups while the teacher provides coaching. Finally, the teacher leads the class in a debriefing session to evaluate their performances and interpretations, which prepares students to give positive feedback to their classmates in student-led Readers Theater groups.

**MATERIALS:** ⊙ The book *Fox at School* by Edward Marshall (Puffin)

⊙ Copies of the script "Fox Escapes" for every student in your class or group (See Appendix, page 87)

## Preparation

Practice reading aloud "Fox Escapes" from Marshall's *Fox at School* (1983) as you would read any story to the class. Write down plans for two groups who will prepare and perform the script for each other. As you organize these groups, consider who will work well together. Also plan how you will assign roles. Because students will not have much time to practice independently, ensure success by assigning the longer or more difficult parts to the strongest readers (e.g., the narrator, Fox) and the more expressive parts (e.g., Carmen, Miss Moon, Fox) to outgoing students. Plan for shy students or weaker readers to read in groups.

## Teaching the Lesson

**1.** Read the story "Fox Escapes" using appropriate expression, asking students to predict the events and explain their predictions. As you read, point out the differences between what characters say and how they are really feeling. For example, the pictures show that Miss Moon is obviously scared to go down the slide, even though she says she's not afraid.

*continued . . .*

2. Explain that students will be working in two groups to perform "Fox Escapes." Hand out scripts and give students a few minutes to read them independently, helping with difficult words.

3. Break students into two groups and assign roles to individuals or groups of students. Give students a few minutes to read through their own parts, reminding them to think about how the character would talk and act and to use their voices and faces to show the character's feelings.

4. Give groups about ten minutes to read through the script together and plan their actions. Make the book available to students as a resource for interpreting the story. Coach them to use the illustrations to plan their actions and facial expressions (e.g., "Look how the principal is standing in this scene.")

5. Gather the class together and have the groups perform for each other.

6. After both groups have performed, congratulate the students on their first performance. Then lead a whole-class debriefing session in which students talk about what it was like to practice and perform. Start with general questions, such as:

   ⊙ What did it feel like to perform for your classmates?

   ⊙ What was the most fun role or line?

   ⊙ Was there any role or line that was difficult to act out?

   ⊙ What kinds of simple props would be helpful for performing this script?

After you ask these general questions, move to more specific comments about the performances. Keep the feedback positive by pointing out examples of expressive reading and effective actions (e.g. "I like the way Roberto used his eyes when Fox said, 'I don't care for this,'" and "Did you notice the way Kelly read Carmen's lines with the exclamation points?"). Then ask students to give some similar positive examples (e.g., "What were some other effective things you noticed?").

# Incorporating Readers Theater Into Your Language Arts Program

Once you've carried out the introductory lessons described above, there are almost unlimited options for weaving Readers Theater into your language arts program. You might decide to follow the basic schedules described in the next section, or a variation on them like the ones described later in the chapter.

## BASIC PRACTICE AND PERFORMANCE SCHEDULES

The two basic schedules for reading, rehearsing, and performing described in this section are based on suggestions from the Readers Theater research discussed in Chapter 1. For full-length scripts like *The Boy Who Cried Wolf*, I recommend a five-day cycle of read aloud, practice and rehearsal, and performance. (See Box 3-2.) For shorter scripts (e.g., speeches, songs, poetry, and short stories like the ones from *Fox at School*), a three-day cycle works well. (See Box 3-3.)

44

Box 3-2

# A Five-Day Schedule for Full-Length Scripts

**PREPARATION:** Write or select scripts based on students' interests, topics of study in the classroom, and reading levels.

## Schedule

*Day 1:* The teacher reads aloud the books for enjoyment and discussion, and to provide a model of fluency. Books may be read throughout the day or in one sitting. Discuss the characters, motives, and actions, and let students choose the script they want to perform. (Use a sign-up sheet, or draw names and let students choose as their names are drawn.) Give each student a copy of the script to practice independently. They should read through the script before they leave for the day, asking for help with words as needed, and practice it at home.

*Day 2:* Students practice reading scripts in their groups. Each student should take a different part for each reading to provide more practice in reading and so that every student is ready to play any part in case someone is absent on performance day. The teacher moves from group to group, giving feedback and support on fluency and interpretation. While students are practicing, model and offer specific feedback about reading and interpreting. For example, simply telling students to read with more expression is not always helpful. Instead, help students interpret their specific character and decide how to portray that character through voice and actions (e.g., "You're the troll. He's mean, big, and gruff. Show me the voice and face you would use."). Remind students to use the book on which the script is based as a resource.

*Day 3:* Students continue to practice in groups with teacher support. At the end of the time, assign roles (or let students negotiate role choices). Students highlight their parts on their personal copies of the script and practice their own parts at home. Students decide if simple props or costumes are needed.

*Day 4:* Students rehearse, reading their assigned parts, to prepare for the next day's performance. Groups decide who will introduce the characters, where the characters will stand, and what kinds of actions and simple props will be needed. Groups go through a "dry run." The teacher is available for support and advice.

*Day 5:* Groups perform for the class and/or for other audiences. The teacher leads students in an oral debriefing session after all groups have performed.

It is important to remember that, as in all group and independent work, students and teachers will need time to plan and establish routines and learn appropriate behavior. It may take several weeks of explaining, role modeling, and guided practice before such activities run smoothly. As students learn what is needed to prepare for a successful performance, they are motivated to work and practice together productively. This frees the teacher to move around from group to group, listening and offering instruction and feedback as students practice.

As with any instructional approach, you may find it necessary to modify some of the

# A Three-Day Schedule for Short Scripts

**PREPARATION:** Students choose poems or scripts based on scenes from novels or short stories with the teacher's advice and support. (After the students have worked with published poems or prepared scripts, they may use scripts or poems that they have written.)

## Schedule

*Day 1:* The teacher reads aloud the text upon which the scripts are based. (For older students or more experienced readers, students can read the texts themselves.) Assign students to groups and roles or allow them to choose or negotiate, and let students practice their parts silently. (When using poetry, help groups decide how to divide the text into parts for individual reading.)

*Day 2:* In their groups, students read their assigned parts orally in preparation for performance, offering one another constructive feedback and help with difficult words. The teacher also gives feedback to each group on fluency and interpretation. Students decide if simple actions or props are needed.

*Day 3:* Students are given additional practice time if needed, and then each group performs. Lead students in an oral "debriefing" at the end of the performances.

procedures to make Readers Theater work best for your students. For example, there will certainly be some differences across grade levels. Primary teachers will usually read the books aloud before students work with the scripts, while upper-grade students might read the books individually, in partners, or in small groups. Older students might be able to take more responsibility for managing their groups but may need more support with difficult stories or if group conflicts arise. Younger students may be able to manage their own groups once they have had time to learn the procedures.

*Mrs. Bedard gives these boys tips on character interpretation and voice projection as they get ready for their performance.*

Also, keep in mind that students who are shy or insecure, students who are learning English, and those who need extra help with reading might need more teacher support or other modifications before working in small groups to perform scripts for the class. There are many options for easing these students into Readers Theater. (See Box 3-4.) Finally, Readers Theater can be overused, so pay attention to students' reactions, and take a break if needed.

## Tips for Students Who Need Extra Support

⊙ *Provide extra practice with the teacher.* Work with students individually or in a small group, giving them extra support and encouragement, until they are ready to join with other students.

⊙ *Group students for choral reading.* Use scripts with choral parts and/or let students read parts in pairs or groups. Sebesta (2003) recommends using a book like *Green Eggs and Ham* (Seuss, 1960). A stronger reader or the teacher can play the part of Sam-I-Am while the group reads the chorus parts ("I do not like Green Eggs and Ham. I do not like them Sam-I-Am").

⊙ *Choose cumulative texts.* The role of Sam-I-Am in *Green Eggs and Ham* is a good choice for struggling readers who want to try a major role. Because the text is cumulative (each new episode repeats and builds on the previous one), the reading is less demanding than a text without repetition. Mem Fox's *Hattie and the Fox* (1992), Linda Williams's *The Old Lady Who Was Not Afraid of Anything* (1988) (see Appendix, page 97, for the script), and Harve Zemach's *The Judge* (1969) (great for older students) also have cumulative parts.

⊙ *Assign simple parts.* Use books that have some short, easy parts, such as one or two words repeated multiple times. *The Little Old Lady Who Was Not Afraid of Anything* has several such parts (the shoes that go "Clomp, Clomp," the pants that go "Wiggle, Wiggle"), as does Ann McGovern's retelling of *Too Much Noise* (1967) and Marjorie Cuyler's *That's Good! That's Bad!* (1996).

⊙ *Adapt scripts.* Shorten or simplify a part to make it easier to read. For example, narrator or character parts can be split for multiple readers.

# VARIATIONS ON BASIC SCHEDULES

How you use Readers Theater will depend on your instructional goals. The basic schedules work well for using Readers Theater as a regular part of the curriculum, but there are almost unlimited alternatives. Every time I talk to a teacher who uses Readers Theater, I learn a different way of organizing. In this section, I describe some ways that teachers in grades 3 through 6 have used Readers Theater.

## Guided Reading

Mrs. Buchanan, a third-grade teacher, incorporates Readers Theater into her guided reading groups. This way, she can work with one group at a time and give students more support and feedback. While Mrs. B. works with the Readers Theater group, other students are reading or writing independently. Readers Theater is used throughout the year with one group preparing and presenting a performance each week. Mrs. Buchanan explains, "Everyone looks forward to their turn to perform. They never get tired of it."

## Thematic Units

Sixth-grade teacher Mr. Cordova alternates Readers Theater with other reading instruction approaches. Every month, he does a one-week Readers Theater unit. He chooses three or four scripts that are related in topic or theme (e.g., stories about pets) and begins the week by reading the books aloud. Students choose the book they want to perform and then work in groups to rehearse and prepare for Friday performances while Mr. Cordova moves from group to group, providing support and feedback. Throughout the year, students gradually take on more responsibility for their performances, reading the books in small groups and writing their own scripts.

## Literature Circles

Mrs. Williams does two six-week Readers Theater units per year with her fifth graders. In the first unit, the class focuses on reading fluently and learning to perform using scripts from Mrs. Williams's collection. In the second unit, Readers Theater is integrated with literature circles, and the students write scripts based on their favorite scenes from the novels they are reading.

## Content Areas

Mr. Liu uses Readers Theater as a culmination to inquiry units in his fourth-grade science and social studies classes. Groups of students spend two or more weeks researching and writing about a topic. Then they prepare a Readers Theater script to present the information they have gathered in a format like the following:

**Reader #1:** Good afternoon! Welcome to our presentation called . . .

**All:** Working Dogs.

**Reader #2:** Today you will learn about some of the different jobs dogs can do and how important they are to our lives.

**Reader #3:** We've all heard about Dalmations who ride with firefighters to the scene of a fire and seeing eye dogs who help the blind. But dogs can do lots of other jobs, too.

**Reader #4:** Some dogs specialize in helping sick people. Researchers have found that animals can actually help people heal faster after an operation.

# Final Thought

As this chapter has shown, a little organization and teaching can go a long way in setting the stage for using Readers Theater in your classroom. I hope I've convinced you that Readers Theater will be a great addition to your language arts program, no matter what your situation or grade level.

In the next chapter, you'll read about the almost unlimited variety of materials you can use for Readers Theater performances. Students can perform poetry, songs, or read books aloud. Alternatively, you can use ready-to-perform scripts, which are available on the Internet and in commercial book collections. I also offer step-by-step directions for writing original scripts and tips for helping students adapt scripts from literature.

# Chapter 4

# Finding and Creating Scripts for Readers Theater

About ten years ago, I started an after-school tutoring program in a local school. The tutors for the program, who were students at the university where I teach, had done a terrific job of finding materials that their students were interested in reading, and most students had made great strides in their reading achievement and motivation. However, there were still a handful of students who were dead set against anything having to do with reading. We had already used Readers Theater with success, but only for end-of-program performances. To try to reach those resistant readers, I began giving tutors the option of using Readers Theater informally. The tutors and I were delighted with the results. Even the most resistant readers were asking to read scripts in every session, and several were taking home scripts to read with their friends and families.

Box 4-1

# Readers Theater on the Web

***Aaron Shepard's RT Page*** (www.aaronshep.com/rt)

Aaron Shepard, children's author and former actor, links his Readers Theater Web page to his children's literature Web site. Books and scripts are sold on the site, but there are also free scripts and tips on reading, rehearsing, and writing scripts. The scripts, appropriate for ages 8–15, include mostly funny stories, fantasy, and folk tales from various cultures. There is even a set of free, downloadable practice sheets written at a variety of difficulty levels to use in teaching students to write scripts.

***Reader's Theater Scripts*** (www.geocities.com/rtscripts)

This site includes a large collection of downloadable scripts aimed at a wide range of ages.

***Readers Theatre @ Pauline Johnson*** (http://pajps.haltonbe.on.ca/)

This Web site presents a "detailed look at how one elementary school (Pauline Johnson Elementary) has used Reader's Theater, with a 'how-to' section for others wishing to do the same."

***Scripts for Schools*** (www.scriptsforschools.com/1.html)

On this site, Lois Walker—a former university drama teacher and producer—describes the benefits of Readers Theater and offers tips for primary grades, middle grades, and teens on this site. Many Readers Theater links and free scripts are included.

***Laura Kump*** (www.readinglady.com/readers_theater *or* http://cpanel.servdns.net/~readingl/Readers_Theater/index.html) Laura Kump is a reading specialist and staff developer. Her Web site includes many free scripts.

***Readers Theater With Sam Sebesta***
(www.teachervision.com/tv/resources/specialist/ssebesta2.html)
Sebesta, a teacher educator and former teacher, includes frequently asked questions, pitfalls, tips for performing, and book recommendations on his site. He also describes how to modify Readers Theater for students with special needs.

***Classroom Theater*** (www.fictionteachers.com)

Children's author Bruce Lansky includes free scripts, lesson plans, and information on this Web site.

***Lisa Blau on Readers Theater*** (http://lisablau.com/plays.html)

Children's author and educational consultant Lisa Blau passed away recently. She leaves a legacy of devotion to education. Her Web site offers Readers Theater books for sale and a "free script of the month." Her topics include science and history as well as folk tales and literature.

I soon found that I needed more sources for scripts, so I looked for books, searched on the Internet, and enlisted my friends who were teachers and educators of teachers to help build a collection of adapted scripts that we could all use. Our students, from elementary- to university-level, also began adapting books and creating original works for Readers Theater. Our joint collection now includes hundreds of scripts. In this chapter, I describe how to find and create scripts for Readers Theater, including performance-ready resources (scripts that can be downloaded from Web sites, books of plays, poetry, and books that can be performed without adaptation). I also include directions for teachers and students to adapt published books for Readers Theater scripts.

# Using Performance-Ready Scripts

## INTERNET RESOURCES

So many people are convinced of the value of Readers Theater that they want to share the wealth. There are numerous Web sites devoted to or related to Readers Theater that offer scripts that can be purchased or downloaded for free. The easiest way to find scripts on the Web is to conduct a search with the key words "readers theater." Spend some time searching and reviewing sites. With a little digging, you can find a wealth of free scripts, as well as tips for using Readers Theater with your students. In the last search I conducted, I found numerous commercial sites and hundreds of Web listings sponsored by universities, classrooms, schools, districts, and educational organizations. The sites included instructions for downloading and/or ordering scripts, informational articles, lists of books, instructional tips, links to other sources, and research and testimonials about using Readers Theater.

Mrs. Bedard, the fifth-grade teacher described in Chapter 1, found the script for *Zachary Beaver* (Holt, 1999) as she was searching for instructional activities for the book. She also found scripts for other books, including *Flying Solo* (Fletcher, 1998) on an educational site called the Little Red Schoolhouse (http://www.suzyred.com/readertheater.html).

Even Web sites that sell scripts often include free scripts to whet your appetite, as well as information about Readers Theater and helpful tips for conducting it. I've listed some sites in box 4-1. Be aware that any information you find could disappear into cyberspace at any time, so be sure to note good ideas and download scripts to your computer's hard drive so you'll have them for later.

## COMMERCIAL COLLECTIONS

Many books include collections of Readers Theater scripts that can be useful if you are looking for ready-to-copy scripts as a starting point for Readers Theater. Box 4-2 lists some recommended books. If you want scripts that

---

**Box 4-2**

### Commercial Collections of Scripts

*You're on! Seven Plays in English and Spanish* by L. Carlsen (William Morrow).

*Theatre for Young Audiences: 20 Great Plays for Children* by A. J. Coleman (St. Martin's).

*Show Time at the Polk Street School: Plays You Can Do Yourself* by P. R. Giff (Bantam Doubleday Dell).

*Immigration* by S. J. Glasscock (Scholastic).

*Great Moments in Science: Experiments and Readers Theatre* by K. Haven (Teacher Ideas Press).

*Stories on Stage: Scripts for Reader's Theater* by A. Shepard & H. W. Wilson (H.W. Wilson).

focus on a certain topic to accompany an instructional unit, such as immigration or famous scientists, such collections can be a good resource. Other recommended collections here are either based on children's books or are written by children's authors and can be a good way to expose students to works of literature. For example, Lori Carlsen's *You're On: Seven Plays in English and Spanish* (1999) includes works by Latino authors. Patricia Reilly Giff's collection (1992) is based on her popular Kids of the Polk Street School chapter book series.

## CHILDREN'S BOOKS

Web resources, commercial collections, and other published materials are a good way to ease into Readers Theater. However, most teachers (and students) eventually find that using the children's books in their own classrooms is more satisfying and motivating. Two basic categories of children's books can be used for Readers Theater: those that can be performed with little or no modification of the text, and those that require reformatting into scripts. Books within both categories are, for the most part, familiar and popular children's titles that can be found in your school or classroom library.

In the two sections immediately following, I discuss performance-ready books. Many teachers start off their experience with Readers Theater using these kinds of books. However, they soon find that they need to expand their repertoire and they supplement by writing their own scripts based on children's literature. Most of the remainder of the chapter is therefore devoted to this key element of Readers Theater.

*This is the Readers Theater shelf in a third-grade classroom library. It comprises both books and scripts; each script is kept in a folder, next to the book it accompanies. Before placing a script in the Readers Theater center, the teacher reads the book out loud to the class.*

### Poetry and Other Lyrical Texts

Poetry, speeches, and song lyrics provide performance-ready formats and meaningful materials to interpret for Readers Theater performances. All lend themselves to choral reading as well as independent and small-group performance. Alexandra Hanson-Harding's book *Great American Speeches, Grades 4–8* (1999) includes short speeches appropriate for performance by students in the intermediate grades. Several of Raffi's songs (e.g., "Down By the Bay") have been turned into picture books. For songs more popular with intermediate-grade students, encourage students to bring the lyrics from their favorite songs. (Of course, you will check to be sure they are appropriate for school.) For performances, students can either read the lyrics like poetry or sing along with the music after practicing.

Joanna Cole and Stephanie Calmenson's collections of rhymes (e.g., *Miss Mary Mack and Other Children's Street Rhymes*, 1992) are excellent for choral reading and for inexperienced performers because they are catchy and familiar. Poetry is also great for modeling and practicing interpretive reading. Some of my favorite funny poems are "Mother doesn't want a dog" in Judith Viorst's book *If I Was in Charge of the World and Other Worries* (1981) and Jack Prelutsky's "Homework, oh Homework" in *The New Kid on the Block* (1984). Shel Silverstein's poems are also great fun for performance. Collections with more serious poems include Medina's *My Name is Jorge on Both Sides of the River* (1999) and Nye's *This Same Sky: A Collection of Poems From Around the World* (1992).

---

**Box 4-3**

# Poetry for Readers Theater

* *Street Music: City Poems* by A. Adoff (HarperCollins).

*All the Small Poems and Fourteen More* by N. Babbit (Farrar, Strauss, & Giroux).

* *Thirteen Moons on Turtle's Back: A Native American Year of Moons* by J. Bruchac & J. London (Lawrence Hill).

* *Animals, Animals* by E. Carle (Scholastic).

*Miss Mary Mack and Other Children's Street Rhymes* by J. Cole & S. Calmenson (Beech Tree).

*Love that Dog* by S. Creech (HarperTrophy).

* *I am Phoenix: Poems for Two Voices* by P. Fleischman (Harper & Row).

* *Joyful noise: Poems for Two Voices* by P. Fleischman (Harper & Row).

*Big talk: Poems for Four Voices* by P. Fleischman (Candlewick).

*Night on Neighborhood Street* by E. Greenfield (Dial).

* *Marvelous Math: A Book of Poems* by L. B. Hopkins (Simon & Schuster).

*More Surprises* by L. B. Hopkins (Harper & Row).

*You read to me, I'll read to you: Very short stories to read together* by M. A. Hoberman (Little, Brown).

*The Dream Keeper and Other Poems* by L. Hughes (Knopf).

*Soap Soup, and Other Verses* by K. Kuskin (HarperCollins).

* *My Name is Jorge on Both Sides of the River* by J. Medina (Wordsong/Boyds Mills Press).

* *This Same Sky: A Collection of Poems From Around the World* by N. S. Nye (Simon & Schuster).

*It's Halloween* by J. Prelutsky (William Morrow).

*The New Kid on the Block* by J. Prelutsky (Scholastic).

*I Saw You in the Bathtub and Other Folk Rhymes* by A. Schwartz (Harper & Row).

*A Light in the Attic* by S. Silverstein (Harper & Row).

*Neighborhood Odes* by G. Soto (Harcourt Brace).

*If I Were in Charge of the World* by J. Viorst (Aladdin).

* *I Never Saw Another Butterfly: Children's Drawings and Poems From Terezin Concentration Camp* by H. Volavkova (Schocken).

* Can be used to support content areas

Paul Fleischman's collections of poems are for multiple voices (1988, 1985, 2000). Some parts of the poems are meant to be read independently and others simultaneously, so students have to follow their parts carefully and stay with their group. Fleischman's books are good for older children. For younger children, try Mary Ann Hoberman's *You Read to Me, I'll Read to You: Very Short Stories to Read Together* (2001).

Poetry can also be used to introduce and support content area topics, including science, social and cultural studies, and even mathematics. Box 4-3 lists a variety of poetry collections and novels told in verse.

## Children's Books That Can Be Performed as Written

Some books can be performed without changing a word. Some are written as scripts, such as *Hey Little Ant* (Hoose & Hoose, 1998). Others, including Raschka's *Yo! Yes?* (1993) and McNaughton's *Suddenly!* (1998) contain only a few words, but lend themselves to dramatic reading. Tales written in verse, such as Frances Minters's *Cinder-Elly* (1994), excerpted below, are also excellent to perform.

> Once upon a time
> Or so they tell me
> There was a girl
> Called Cinder-Elly
>
> Elly was good
> And she was pretty
> She lived with her folks
> In New York City
>
> *That girl was so good!*

Cumulative stories, in which each event builds on the previous one, can also be performed as written. They are great for Readers Theater because of the repeated text. Examples of familiar cumulative stories are "The House That Jack Built" and "There Was An Old Lady Who Swallowed a Fly." Harve Zemach's *The Judge* (1969) is a cumulative book that's popular with students in the intermediate grades:

> Please let me go Judge
> I didn't know Judge
> That what I did was against the law
> I just said what I saw.
>
> A horrible thing is coming this way
> Creeping closer day by day
> Its eyes are scary; its tale is hairy
> I tell you Judge, we all better pray!

Each episode repeats the basic details about the "horrible thing" ("its eyes are scary; its tale is hairy") and adds additional ones ("its paws have claws, it snaps its jaws;" "it growls, it groans, it chews up stones"). This repetition provides a fun, authentic way to reread the same text, and this book is much loved by students. Box 4-4 lists other books that can be read straight from the book or retyped as scripts.

# Scripting Children's Literature

One of the greatest benefits of Readers Theater is its connection to books, and every teacher and class has favorite books that are unlikely to be published in script form. When Readers Theater is based on books in your classroom, your students want to read those books. Further, because no two teachers teach in the same way, no published collection will have quite the right books and topics for the units you plan to study. Finally, when students perform teacher-written scripts, they are more likely to try writing scripts themselves, either with help or on their own. This is when the full potential of Readers Theater is realized, as an approach to reading, writing, and learning across the curriculum.

The next section provides some things to consider when choosing and writing scripts. See Box 4-5 for tips on scripting, too.

> **Box 4-4**
>
> ## Books That Can Be Performed as Written
>
> *That's Good! That's Bad!* by M. Cuyler (Owlet).
>
> *Fortunately!* by R. Charlip (Scott Foresman).
>
> *Charlie and the Chocolate Factory: A Play* by R. Dahl (Puffin).
>
> *Hey, Little Ant* by P. Hoose & H. Hoose (Tricycle Press).
>
> *Suddenly! A Preston Pig Story* by C. McNaughton (Voyager).
>
> *Cinder-Elly* by F. Minters (Viking).
>
> *Sleepless Beauty* by F. Minters (Puffin).
>
> *Yo! Yes?* by C. Raschka (Scholastic).
>
> *Yo, Hungry Wolf! A Nursery Rap* by D. Vozer (Doubleday).
>
> *The Judge* by H. Zemach (Collins).

## BOOK CHOICE

The two most important rules of thumb for choosing literature to adapt for Readers Theater is that the script should lend itself to dramatic interpretation and should be interesting for performers and the audience. According to Strecker, Roser, and Marinez (1999), texts chosen for performance should have straightforward plots that present characters working through dilemmas. In his "Tips on Scripting" for Readers Theater (www.aaronshep.com/rt/tipsl.html), Aaron Shepard recommends using stories that are "simple and lively, with lots of dialogue or action, and with not too many scenes or characters." As I will discuss later in this chapter, information books can also be effectively adapted for Readers Theater.

Some books are less suitable for Readers Theater because their illustrations carry much of the story's weight. For example, the illustrations in books like William Steig's *Spinky Sulks* (1991), Peggy Rathman's *Officer Buckle and Gloria* (1995), and Chris Van Allsburg's *Jumanji* (1981), are essential to the book's meaning, so the information would be too difficult to convey in a script without complex scenery and costumes. It's better to use books like these for Read Alouds and other situations in which the illustrations can be seen.

## SCRIPT LENGTH

In my experience, about three to four typewritten pages in a 14-point clear font (such as Arial or Geneva) is a good maximum script length. A script of this length should take no longer than 10 or 15 minutes to perform. If a book is too long, you can modify it in a way that's appropriate for the book. For example, you can script only one or two scenes or leave off the ending and invite the audience to guess what happens and to read the rest of the book to find out (see *The Three Little Pigs: Nacho, Tito, and Miguel* in the Appendix, page 82, for an example). When a story has long stretches of narration, you can condense it, as long as you leave in the information that's most important for understanding the book. Script length will depend on the text, of course, but it is generally better to use shorter scripts for younger and/or less experienced readers, as well as for younger audiences.

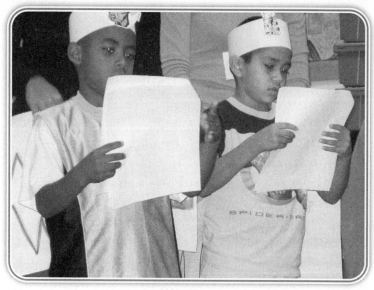

It's the day they have been waiting for, and these boys are nervous but excited. They are performing their first Readers Theater for an audience of teachers, school friends, and families.

## QUALITY CONTROL

Before distributing scripts for performance, evaluate them. Put yourself in the place of the audience; read over the script to be sure it isn't boring. If you are working with a new script, be open to modifying it after students read through it. Ask students for suggestions. If they put themselves in the place of the audience and help you revise a script so that it "makes sense," it requires them to do some very sophisticated thinking. This builds reading comprehension and writing skills, and provides an entrée into their own script writing.

> **Box 4-5**
>
> ### Tips for Building Your Readers Theater Collection
>
> ⊙ Always be on the lookout for books that can be adapted for Readers Theater.
>
> ⊙ As you read books aloud, ask your students to consider whether it would be a good choice for Readers Theater and why.
>
> ⊙ To get the most out of Readers Theater, enlist the support of your colleagues. Share books, scripts, and ideas.

# Guidelines for Adapting Different Kinds of Books

## SERIES BOOKS

Series books and other collections that feature the same characters are excellent for beginning scriptwriters and performers because the familiar plot structures, language, and characters give students a built-in source of support for reading. This allows them to focus on

## Adapting a Short Story for Readers Theater

| Text | Script |
|------|--------|
| Carmen, Dexter, and Fox were on their way to school. | **Narrator:** Carmen, Dexter, and Fox were on their way to school. |
| "I'm going to be a pilot when I grow up," said Carmen. | **Carmen:** I'm going to be a pilot when I grow up. |
| "I think I'll be a cowboy," said Dexter. | **Dexter:** I think I'll be a cowboy. |
| "What about you, Fox?" said Carmen. | **Carmen:** What about you, Fox? |
| "I'm going to be a teacher," said Fox. | **Fox:** I'm going to be a teacher. |
| "You're not serious," said Carmen. | **Carmen:** You're not serious. |
| "It's an easy job," said Fox. | **Fox:** It's an easy job. |
| The next morning Fox was in for a little surprise. | **Narrator:** The next morning Fox was in for a little surprise. |
| "I must be away for a few minutes," said Miss Moon. "And I am putting Fox in charge." | **Miss Moon:** I must be away for a few minutes, and I'm putting Fox in charge. |
| "Hot dog!" said Fox. | **Fox:** Hot dog! |

interpretation and expression. The characters, language, and content grow more familiar with each book in the series a student reads. As a result, these books can help increase the confidence of even challenged readers (Worthy, 1996). As Margaret Mackey (1990) put it, "even a reader inexperienced in an absolute sense has the opportunity to behave like an experienced reader." Many students grab on to a series or collection and read every book, and this helps to build fluency.

Box 4-6 illustrates how I adapted a story from *Fox at School* (Marshall, 1983) with few changes to the original text. First, I chose a story with plenty of dialogue and characters that I thought would be fun to perform. Every line of dialogue is important in this story, but the narration can be cut back to include only the lines that are needed to provide important information. For example, I decided to use the first sentence—"Carmen, Dexter, and Fox, were on their way to school"—because it introduced the characters and gave the setting of the story. I chose a later sentence—"The next morning Fox was in for a little surprise"—because it signaled a time change. Throughout the story, I omitted the words, "Carmen said,"

### Series Books and Collections for Readers Theater

*Arthur* by M. Brown (Little, Brown).

*Fox* by E. Marshall (Puffin).

*Junie B. Jones* series by B. Parks (Random House).

*George and Martha* by J. Marshall (Houghton Mifflin).

*Black Lagoon* by M. Thaler (Scholastic).

*Marvin Redpost* series by L. Sachar (Random House).

*Amber Brown* series by Paula Danziger (Scholastic).

Box 4-8

# Fairy Tales, Transformations, and Variants

*The Principal's New Clothes* by S. Calmenson (Scholastic).

*The Chocolate Touch* by P. Catling (Bantam).

*The Korean Cinderella* by S. Climo (HarperTrophy).

*Prince Cinders* by B. Cole (G. P. Putnam's Sons).

*Red Riding Hood* by B. deRegniers (Aladdin).

*Jack and the Beanstalk* by B. deRegniers (Aladdin).

*Ruby* by M. Emberley (Little, Brown).

*The Three Little Pigs and the Fox* by W. Hooks (MacMillan).

*The Boy Who Cried Wolf* by F. Littledale (Scholastic).

*Yeh Shen: A Cinderella story from China* by A. Louie (Philomel).

*The Three Little Javelinas* by S. Lowell (Northland).

*Red Riding Hood* by J. Marshall (Dial).

*The Three Little Pigs* by J. Marshall (Dial).

*The Rough-face Girl* by R. Martin (Putnam).

*Cinder-Elly* by F. Minters (Scholastic).

*Sleepless Beauty* by F. Minters (Scholastic).

*Cinderella* by C. Perrault (Puffin).

*Stone Soup* by T. Ross (Dial).

*The Boy Who Cried Wolf* by T. Ross (Puffin).

**Los Tres Cerdos/The Three Little Pigs: Nacho, Tito, and Miguel* by B. Salinas (Piñata).

*The Talking Eggs* by R. D. San Souci (Scholastic).

*Smoky Mountain Rose: An Appalachian Cinderella* by A. Schroeder (Dial).

*The Stinky Cheese Man and Other Fairly Stupid Tales* by J. Scieszka (Viking).

*The Frog Prince Continued* by J. Scieszka (Viking).

*The True Story of the Three Little Pigs* by J. Scieszka (Viking).

*Upside Down Tales: Cinderella* by R. Shorto (Citadel Press).

*Mufaro's Beautiful Daughters: An African Tale* by J. Steptoe (Lothrop, Lee & Shepard).

*The Three Little Wolves and the Big Bad Pig* by E. Trivizas (Margaret K. McElderry).

*Ugh* by A. Yorinks (Farrar, Straus & Giroux).

*Lon Po Po* by E. Young (Philomel).

* Script included in this book

"said Fox," and so on, because the characters themselves will do the speaking in the Readers Theater performance and this makes those lines unnecessary. Finally, I typed the story in Readers Theater format, as shown in the second column of Box 4-6. The rest of the script, along with scripts of two other stories from the same book, is included in the Appendix (see Appendix, page 77). The series and collections listed in Box 4-7 are easy to script and read, yet sophisticated enough to capture students' interest.

# Fairy Tales, Transformations, and Variants

Picture book versions of folk and fairy tales (e.g., Paul Galdone's *The Little Red Hen*) can be scripted with few modifications by turning dialogue into speaking parts and description into narration. Many intermediate-grade teachers regularly teach a unit on fairy tales that includes transformations and variants, which are also effective for Readers Theater. *Transformations* are retellings of familiar fairy tales in which one or more elements of the story is altered, usually for comic effect. Examples include Susan Lowell's *The Three Little Javelinas* (a three pigs story set in the Southwest), Jon Scieszka's *The Stinky Cheese Man* (based on the Gingerbread Man story) and Patrick Catling's novel *The Chocolate Touch* (a modern-day King Midas story about the hazards of loving chocolate too much). *Variants* are legends, folk tales, or fairy tales from different cultures, such as Ed Young's *Lon Po Po*, a Chinese variant of the Red Riding Hood story. (See Box 4-8 for a list of fairy tales, transformations, and variants.)

A good way to organize a fairy tale unit is to read or have students tell a familiar version of a story they know and then compare it to variants. For example, students probably know the story of Cinderella. Ask them to retell it, then read Rafe Martin's *The Rough-face Girl*, an Algonquin version of the tale, or Shirley Climo's *The Korean Cinderella*, as well as a transformation such as Arthur Yorink's *Ugh*, a prehistoric Cinderella tale with a male protagonist.

To adapt a fairy tale for Readers Theater, I follow the same basic procedure that I use for scripting short stories like the Fox stories. For example, in *The Boy Who Cried Wolf* (see Appendix, page 79), I used all of the lines of narration (except lines such as "Tom cried," and "shouted the hunters") because they provide important story information. In *Los Tres Cerdos/The Three Little Pigs: Nacho, Tito, and Miguel*, I omitted the last few scenes and added an invitation to the audience to predict the end of the story and then read the book to evaluate their predictions (see Appendix, page 82).

# More Complex Adaptations

As you gain more confidence in writing scripts, you will be ready to graduate to less straightforward adaptations using materials like novels, chapter books, and information texts.

## Novels and Chapter Books

Box 4-9 shows how I adapted a scene from *How to Eat Fried Worms* (Rockwell, 1973) for Readers Theater. A major goal of adapting a novel for Readers Theater is to entice the audience to read it, so I started by deciding on a scene that would be an attention grabber. I chose the first scene in the book because it sets up the book's premise, a bet among four boys over whether one of them will eat 15 worms for fifty dollars. Next, I read the scene carefully and began marking the parts that I wanted to include and those that I thought could be left out. (The italicized text in the first column is omitted in the script version.) The opening of a novel or chapter book often includes a lot of description to introduce the characters and setting, as this one does. However, too much narration can bog down a script, so I looked for parts that could be omitted to focus the script more tightly on the setup of the bet. As you'll see in column one, I left out a large portion of the first page, on which the boys are talking about what they did the night before. Because it has nothing to do with the bet, I included only a brief mention in the narrator part. I left in virtually all of the dialogue, omitting only those parts that referred to the night before or that were not important for setting up the bet. For example, I left out Billy's question to Tom about whether his mother was going to make him eat the leftover salmon for lunch.

*After you've started doing Readers Theater, you'll find that you—and your students—discover books everywhere that would make good Readers Theater scripts.*

Notice that I also omitted much of the detailed character description (e.g., Alan argued a lot, small knobby-kneed, nervous, gnawing at his thumbnail, his face smudged, his red hair mussed, shirttail hanging out, shoelaces untied). Even though this may seem like important information for interpreting the characters and understanding the story, remember that in Readers Theater, the actors *always read or hear the book before performing a script* and *they always have the book as a reference* when preparing for the performance. Thus, the actors are already familiar with the characters and with other details about the book and can portray this information through their voices and actions, or with simple props, if needed. This is usually far more engaging to an audience than detailed description read by a narrator.

## Information Books

Readers Theater scripts are most often based on fiction books that have a strong plot and interesting dialogue. It seems logical that such scripts would be more appealing for the performers and the audience. Books without dialogue and those that present straightforward information may seem more difficult to adapt. However, if you want to take full advantage of the power of Readers Theater, I highly recommend using information books and materials related to content area topics such as science, history, and math. Conducting Readers Theater based on these is an excellent way to motivate students, improve fluency, and support conceptual knowledge. As mentioned earlier, Readers Theater can be used in content areas as an introduction to new topics, as a motivating way for students to learn new information, and as a way to present research. Further, there are many ways to adapt information text for Readers Theater to make it engaging as a script, as you'll see in the examples that follow. Box 4-10 lists books in a variety of content areas that make good Readers Theater scripts.

Box 4-9

# Scripting a Novel or Chapter Book

| Original Text | Script |
|---|---|
| "Hey, *Tom!* Where were you last night?"<br>"Yeah, you missed it."<br>*Alan and Billy came up the front walk. Tom was sitting on his porch steps, bouncing a tennis ball.*<br>"Old Man Tator caught Joe as we were climbing *through the fence, so we all had to go back, and he made us pile the peaches on his kitchen table, and then he called our mothers."*<br>"Joe's mother hasn't let him out yet.<br>"Where were you?"<br>*Tom stopped bouncing the tennis ball. He was a tall, skinny boy who took his troubles very seriously.*<br>"My mother kept me in."<br>"What for?"<br>"I wouldn't eat my dinner."<br>*Alan sat down on the step below Tom and began to chew his thumbnail.*<br>"What was it?"<br>"Salmon casserole."<br>*Billy flopped down on the grass, chunky, snubnosed, freckled.*<br>"Salmon casserole's not so bad."<br>"Wouldn't she let you eat just two bites?" *asked Alan.* "Sometimes my mother says, well, all right, if I'll just eat two bites."<br>"I wouldn't even eat one."<br>"That's stupid," *said Billy.* "One bite can't hurt you. I'd eat one bite of anything before I'd let them send me up to my room right after supper."<br>*Tom shrugged.*<br>"How about mud?" *Alan asked Billy.* "You wouldn't eat a bite of mud."<br>*Alan argued a lot, small knobby-kneed, nervous, gnawing at his thumbnail, his face smudged, his red hair mussed, shirttail hanging out, shoelaces untied.*<br>"Sure, I would," *Billy said.* "Mud. What's mud? Just dirt with a little water in it. My father says everyone eats a pound of dirt every year anyway."<br>"How about poison?"<br>"That's different." *Billy rolled over on his back.*<br>*"Is your mother going to make you eat the leftovers today at lunch?" he asked Tom.*<br>"She never has before."<br>"How about worms?" *Alan asked Billy.* | **Narrator:** [Show the book and introduce the characters] The title of this book is *How to Eat Fried Worms* and it's written by Thomas Rockwell. This book is about three boys who make a disgusting bet. This Readers Theater is from the first chapter, which is called, "The Bet." When the story opens, Billy and Alan are talking to Tom about what they did the night before.<br><br>**Alan:** Hey, Tom, where were you last night?<br><br>**Tom:** My mother kept me in.<br><br>**Alan:** What for?<br><br>**Tom:** I wouldn't eat my dinner.<br><br>**Alan:** What was it?<br><br>**Tom:** Salmon casserole.<br><br>**Billy:** Salmon casserole's not so bad.<br><br>**Alan:** Yeah. Wouldn't she let you just eat two bites? Sometimes my mother says, well, all right, if I'll just eat two bites.<br><br>**Tom:** I wouldn't eat even one.<br><br>**Billy:** That's stupid. One bite can't hurt you. I'd eat one bite of anything before I'd let them send me up to my room right after supper.<br><br>*(Tom shrugs)*<br><br>**Alan:** *(To Billy)* How about mud? You wouldn't eat a bite of mud.<br><br>**Billy:** Sure I would. Mud. What's mud? Just dirt with a little water in it. My father says everyone eats a pound of dirt every year anyway.<br><br>**Alan:** How about poison?<br><br>**Billy:** That's different.<br><br>**Alan:** How about worms? |

## Information Books for Readers Theater

### Mathematics

*The Doorbell Rang* by P. Hutchins (Greenwillow).

*100 Hungry Ants* by E. J. Pinczes (Houghton Mifflin).

*Sideways Arithmetic from Wayside School* by L. Sachar (Scholastic).

*Math Curse* by J. Scieszka (Viking).

### Social Studies

*Smoky Night* by E. Bunting (Harcourt Brace).

*The Diary of Anne Frank* (93rd ed.) by A. Frank (Harcourt Brace).

*I Have a Dream* by M. L. King (Scholastic).

*Oh, Freedom! Kids Talk About the Civil Rights Movement With the People Who Made it Happen* by C. S. King & L. B. Osborne (Knopf).

*Amazon Diary: The Jungle Adventures of Alex Winters* by H. Talbott (Putnam).

### Science

*\*Micro Monsters: Life Under the Microscope* by C. Maynard (Dorling Kindersley).

*Amazing Poisonous Animals* (Eyewitness Juniors, No. 8) by A. Parsons (Knopf).

*Script included in the Appendix

The simplest way to adapt an information book is to divide the text into short segments of one to four lines, depending on the content of the text and the number of readers. The example in Box 4-11 is from *Cats That Roar* (Weinberger, 2002). The first column shows the original text and the second column shows a simple adapted script. In the third column, a choral part (ALL) is added to highlight interesting or exciting parts of the text and to give each reader more parts. Alternatively, the choral part could be read by a group of students or by the rest of the class. This type of adaptation also works well for history books. (Fiction books with sparse dialogue, like the Latino folktale *La Llorona*, retold by Joe Hayes, can be scripted in a similar way.)

Another way to adapt information books is to turn narration into dialogue for the characters in the text. For example, using an adaptation of Maynard's *Micro Monsters: Life Under the Microscope* (1999) (Appendix, page 102), several fourth graders practiced and performed the chapter on "Mighty Mites" for their classmates. The students acted out the roles of itch mites, lice, and other microscopic insects, describing what they did in gory but accurate detail while the audience struggled to keep from turning green. Maynard's book features first-person narration from the bugs' point of view, so it was easy to transform it into dialogue and use the remaining text for narrator and chorus parts. The first column in Box 4-12 shows an excerpt from the chapter on "Mighty Mites" and the second column shows how the text was scripted (adaptation by Gay Ivey).

Box 4-11

## A Straightforward Adaptation of an Informational Text

| Original Text | Script With Four Readers | Script With Choral Part |
|---|---|---|
| *Cats that Roar!*<br><br>It is nighttime. A big cat moves slowly and silently in the forest. It has not eaten in three days. It is very hungry.<br><br>Suddenly, the cat's ears point straight up as it stares into the darkness. It sees a deer many yards away. Without a sound, the big cat creeps toward the deer. As it draws closer, the cat begins to move more quickly. Then, in a single leap, the deer is knocked to the ground. The big cat has made the kill. It will eat well tonight. | **Rdr 1:** It is nighttime. A big cat moves slowly and silently in the forest. It has not eaten in three days. It is very hungry.<br><br>**Rdr 2:** Suddenly, the cat's ears point straight up as it stares into the darkness. It sees a deer many yards away.<br><br>**Rdr 3:** Without a sound, the big cat creeps toward the deer. As it draws closer, the cat begins to move more quickly.<br><br>**Rdr 4:** Then, in a single leap, the deer is knocked to the ground. The big cat has made the kill. It will eat well tonight. | **Rdr 1:** It is nighttime. A big cat moves slowly and silently in the forest.<br><br>**ALL:** It has not eaten in three days. It is very hungry.<br><br>**Rdr 2:** Suddenly, the cat's ears point straight up as it stares into the darkness. It sees a deer many yards away.<br><br>**Rdr 3:** Without a sound, the big cat creeps toward the deer. As it draws closer, the cat begins to move more quickly.<br><br>**Rdr 4:** Then, in a single leap, the deer is knocked to the ground.<br><br>**ALL:** The big cat has made the kill. It will eat well tonight. |

# Having Students Write Scripts

Students learn a great deal about fluency, comprehension, interpretation, literature, content areas, and working in groups from participating in Readers Theater. When students write their own scripts, it adds another dimension. Rather than writing just for the teacher, students write for a very real audience. To write an effective script, students will need to think deeply about how to make their writing both comprehensible and interesting. Start by modeling how to adapt a

*This teacher and student are discussing how to adapt a favorite scene from a short story for a Readers Theater script.*

Box 4-12

# Creating Character Roles From an Informational Text

| Original Text | Script |
|---|---|
| Did you know that more than a million eight-legged, hump-backed creatures are probably living under YOUR bed? We are dust mites—and we'll bet lots of us live all over your home. Any place that is humid and warm suits us just fine.<br><br>Mostly we live in dust, especially in places that trap tufts of it—such as deep carpets, pillows, bedding, and sofas. Dust might seem like a strange place to live. But it isn't if you look at it closely. It is mostly made up of strands of hair, clothes, fibers, carpet fluff, and countless flakes of human skin. And skin flakes are what we mites really love to eat. It's why so many of us crowd together in mattresses and in carpets under beds. For us, these places are just like orchards where millions of delicious skin flakes drop from human beings every day. | **Chorus:** Did you know that more than a million eight-legged, hump-backed creatures are probably living under your bed?<br><br>**Dust Mites:** We are dust mites—and I'll bet lots of us live all over your home. Any place that is humid and warm suits us just fine.<br><br>**Narrator:** Dust mites mostly live in dust, especially in places that trap tufts of it—like deep carpets, pillows, bedding, and sofas. Dust might seem like a strange place to live.<br><br>**Chorus:** But it isn't if you look at it closely.<br><br>**Narrator:** Dust is mostly made up of strands of hair, clothes, fibers, carpet fluff, and countless flakes of human skin.<br><br>**Dust Mite 1:** And skin flakes are we what mites really love to eat. It's why so many of us crowd together in mattresses and in carpets under beds.<br><br>**Dust Mite 2:** For us, these places are just like orchards where millions of delicious skin flakes drop from human beings every day. |

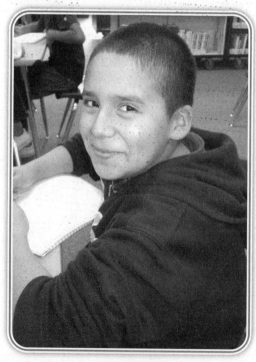

*Adapting books for Readers Theater scripts is a perfect activity for Writing Workshop.*

64

book for Readers Theater and supporting students as they write their own adaptations. This plan describes how to get students going by starting with heavy teacher support and moving toward independence.

# INTRODUCTORY WRITING LESSON

Students' first scripts should be based on books that can be adapted easily. The Fox books by Edward Marshall fit the bill perfectly. This lesson uses the same story "Fox on Stage" from Marshall's *Fox at School* that is also used in the Appendix, page 88.

## LESSON 4–1

# Introducing Script Writing

**GOALS:** To provide students with modeling, support, and guided practice so they will be prepared to adapt scripts on their own and in groups..

**CONTENT:** In this lesson, the teacher models the process of writing a script based on a segment of a short story and then guides students as they adapt the remainder of the story.

**MATERIALS:**
- *Fox at School* by Edward Marshall (Puffin)
- Overhead transparency of each page of the story
- Overhead transparency markers
- Large blank chart paper

## Preparation

Practice reading aloud "Fox on Stage," just as you would read any story to the class.

## Teaching the Lesson

1. Read the story aloud. If students have not already heard it, ask them to predict events and support their predictions. Explain that you will be showing how to write a script based on the story so they will be able to write scripts themselves.

2. Place the transparency of the first page of the story on the overhead projector. Point out the narration ("the part that tells what happens") and the dialogue ("the part that the characters say") in the first two lines and mark each on the transparency:

   {Fox wanted a part in the class play.} (Narration)
   ["We must be fair,"] (Dialogue)
   {said Miss Moon.} (Narration)
   ["Now, let's see who will play the pretty princess] (Dialogue)

3. Ask students to tell you which part is the narration and dialogue in the next few lines. Mark them on the transparency:

*continued . . .*

*Readers Theater for Building Fluency* • Scholastic Teaching Resources

65

She drew out the first name. "The pretty princess will be played by Carmen," announced Miss Moon.

"O, goody!" said Carmen.
"And now for the part of the mean dragon," said Miss Moon.
Fox held his breath.

4. On chart paper, build the script while students watch, explaining every step. Write "narrator" and then the narrator's line, followed by each character's name and then that character's line. Point out that when adapting a script, the writer must decide how much information the audience will need to understand the story without making the performance boring. For example, narration such as "Fox said" is usually omitted. When you have finished scripting the story, read through the script chorally and decide, thinking out loud, if revisions should be made. Your script will look like this:

**Narrator:** Fox wanted a part in the class play.

**Miss Moon:** We must be fair. I'll put everyone's name in a shoe box.
Now, let's see who will play the pretty princess.

**Narrator:** She drew out the first name.

**Miss Moon:** The pretty princess will be played by Carmen.

**Carmen:** O, goody!

**Miss Moon:** And now for the part of the mean dragon.

**Narrator:** Fox held his breath.

**Miss Moon:** The mean dragon will be played by Junior.

**Junior:** I'll do my best.

**Miss Moon:** And now for the part of the handsome prince.

**Narrator:** Fox bit his nails.

**Miss Moon:** That part goes to Fox.

**Fox:** Hot dog!

**Dexter:** Rats.

**Miss Moon:** Everyone else will play flowers and trees.

**Fox:** Gosh. The handsome prince.

5. Let students script the next page of the story independently on their own papers while you do the same on the chart paper. Then compare their versions with yours. Continue scripting page by page until you finish the story.

6. Finally, lead the class in reading the entire script from the chart, and edit if necessary.

*Readers Theater for Building Fluency* • Scholastic Teaching Resources

# WRITING SCRIPTS WITH LESS TEACHER SUPPORT

The lesson should give students enough guidance to write similar scripts with minimum support from you. Continue to provide coaching as students choose books, write, and revise their scripts. It helps if a computer is available for each group so scripts can be edited and refined as needed. For younger students and less-experienced readers, you may choose to stick with the Fox stories, other easy-to-script story collections, and simple fairy tales. See Box 4-13 for suggested books.

If you want to give older students opportunities to adapt different kinds of texts, such as information texts or scenes from novels, use the scripts in the Appendix (along with the books upon which they are based) as models. Aaron Shepard's Web site offers lessons on scripting along with short stories on a variety of levels that students can use for practice. You can also use Mrs. Bedard's idea (mentioned in the Introduction) of having students write summaries of book scenes and then turning them into Readers Theater scripts.

Leave the door open for students to write original scripts inspired by published books. For example, students in a third-grade class wrote and performed an advertisement for "Freckle Juice" based on Judy Blume's book of the same name.

*These girls are collaborating to write an original script based on a book they have read. Because they know they will perform their script for the class, they read it again and again, negotiating, revising, and rehearsing until they are sure their performance will be a hit.*

---

Box 4-13

### Easy-to-Script Books for Readers Theater

Marc Brown's *Arthur* (e.g., *Arthur's Eyes*).

Edward Marshall's *Fox* (e.g., *Fox at School*).

James Marshall's *George and Martha* (e.g., *George and Martha Back in Town*).

James Marshall's fairy tales (e.g., *Red Riding Hood*).

Paul Galdone's fairy tales (e.g., *The Three Billy Goats Gruff*).

Freya Littledale's fairy tales (e.g., *The Boy Who Cried Wolf*).

# Final Thought

If you're like the teachers I know who have discovered Readers Theater, you have probably already started building your collection of scripts and supplies. You've probably discovered some Web sites that aren't in this book, and I bet you can't read a book without thinking about whether it would be a good one for performing. It won't be long before your students are writing scripts spontaneously, or maybe they already are. Have you gone way over your book budget?  Sorry, you have the Readers Theater bug; it spreads quickly, and I don't know of a cure.

Your students have been enjoying performing for each other and their confidence has been building. Now comes the part that's even more fun—inviting audiences to watch your students perform. In the final chapter, I will describe how to prepare for a successful public performance.

# Chapter 5

# Preparing for and Carrying Out Performances for a Real Audience

It's November, and your class has been doing Readers Theater in the classroom since the beginning of the year. You've taught the introductory lessons in Chapter 3, have tried several schedules, and found one that works for you. You've used scripts in the Appendix of this book and have written several of your own. Even your most reluctant students have begun to participate and enjoy performing for the class. Like a soccer team that has practiced and scrimmaged for weeks, they are ready to play a real game. What now? It's time to think about performing for a "real" audience.

There are many things to think about to make a Readers Theater program successful, including deciding how many and which scripts will be performed, which guests to invite to your real performance, how to prepare students for the performances, how to set up the room, and so on. Of course, every situation is different, and things may come up that you have not thought about. Because preparation will help to ensure a successful program, it is helpful to spend time with students planning for their Readers Theater performances.

# Inviting Audience Members and Establishing the Program

With your students, decide whom you will invite to the program. Another class at your grade level or lower is often a good choice. After students have had some experiences with a small audience, you may choose to hold a more formal "performance party" program and invite students' families and, perhaps, the school principal.

Decide on the details of your program, such as the time and place. If you're performing for parents, you might want to choose a time at the beginning of the day so that parents don't have to miss work. For other classes, discuss a good time with the other teacher(s). If you're planning on a large audience, you might want to make arrangements to hold your program in the school library, cafeteria, or auditorium. For a smaller audience, your classroom should work fine.

## INVITATIONS TO THE PERFORMANCE

After the details are set, send an invitation to your audience. Include a brief description of the program, the time, date, and anything you want the audience to know. See Box 5-1 for a sample invitation. Let students decorate invitations with clip art or with their own designs. If you wish to provide light refreshments after the program, finger foods and boxed juices work best. You can ask students to sign up to contribute.

Notice that the total program is quite short. Limiting the performance time to not more than 30 minutes helps young audiences maintain attention. Add about 10 minutes to the overall time for getting the audience settled, providing a quick intermission, and/or serving refreshments.

---

Box 5-1

### Sample Invitation

Dear (Name of invitee),

Please join Miss Garza's class for a Readers Theater performance of some of our favorite stories and books about animals.

Time: 2:00 to 2:40 p.m.

Place: Room 304, Eastwood Elementary

---

## PROGRAMS FOR THE PERFORMANCE

You may choose to type up and copy a program for the audience that includes the title of each performance and performers' names. See Box 5-2 for a sample program.

## Sample Program for a Performance

### *Performance Party Presented by Mrs. Grayson's Class*
**November 17, 2004**

*Welcome families, teachers, and friends. We hope you enjoy the show.*

"Us" from *Where the Sidewalk Ends* by Shel Silverstein
José and Bryan

*Too Much Noise* retold by Ann McGovern
Ariana, Savannah, Ray, Steven, Gloria, Joseph, Alicia, María, Juan, Michael, Mary, Sheldon, Tyrone

*Click Clack Moo: Cows That Type* by Doreen Cronin
Anisa, Jesse, Tia, Gaby, Stephanie, Delia, Mario, Denise, Glenda, José

Favorite jokes by Jesse and Stephanie

Poems for two voices from *I'll Read to You, You Read to Me* by Mary Ann Hoberman
"I Like": Savannah and Christina
"Two Cats": James and Kelly

Original Poems based on *If I Were in Charge of the World* by Judith Viorst
Authors: Glenda and Denise

Song: "The Little Green Frog"
Gloriana and Katie

A Story from *Fox on Wheels* by Edward Marshall
Actors: Delia, Mario, Gabriela, Margaret

*Please join us after the performances for juice and cookies*

# Selecting Scripts

When planning for performances with an audience, let students choose "tried and true" scripts—favorites that they have performed in front of the class. The type of audience will determine how long the total program should be, as well as which scripts you'll use and how many you'll perform. For example, if you will be inviting primary-grade students to the performance, select scripts of interest to that age level and plan for a total program time of about 20 minutes. These 20 minutes might include three to five short scripts (about the length of one of the Fox stories in the Appendix) or one or two longer scripts along with a poem or two along with a quick break for stretching.

Particularly for younger students, consider including some performances that will involve the audience. A great script for audience participation and for younger students is *The Little Old Lady Who Was Not Afraid of Anything* (Williams, 2002) (see Appendix, page 97) or McGovern's *Too Much Noise* (1967), in which the audience can join in as the performers repeat the same phrases throughout the script. The audience can follow the performers' directions and be part of the action in poems like Silverstein's "I'm Being Swallowed By a Boa Constrictor" from *Where the Sidewalk Ends* (1974).

# Reviewing Responsibilities of Performers and Audience Members

Even though students have had experience with an audience (their classmates) during in-class performances, it is helpful to review performance tips and specifically address what will happen when an outside audience watches their performances. Since everyone will be an audience member, discuss audience responsibilities as well. Make a chart like the one in Box 5-3 and post it in or near the Readers Theater performance area. Refer to the chart during rehearsals and before performances as you remind students of their responsibilities. Add others that students come up with as they prepare for performances. Also, post announcements about upcoming performances.

Box 5-3

## Performer and Audience Member Responsibilities

**Performers, remember to:**

*(Before the performance)*

- Read your script many times so you know it well.

- Practice reading your part with expression.

- Plan with your group how to stand and how to move during the performance.

- Designate a performer (usually the narrator) to announce the performance, show the audience the book, and present the performers.

*(During the performance)*

- Face the audience.

- Don't cover your mouth with your script.

- Read loudly so everyone can hear you.

- Read with expression.

- If someone makes a mistake, keep going.

- If the audience is laughing, wait before you continue.

- Smile and remember to have fun.

- Thank the audience for coming.

**Audience members, remember to:**

- Sit quietly and listen attentively.

- Respect the performers.

- If someone makes a mistake, ignore it.

- Clap at the end of the performance.

- Think of ways you can compliment the performers.

72

# PERFORMERS

## Before Performances

Students should practice the script so that they can read every word in their part easily and smoothly. During rehearsals, they should practice reading in a loud, clear voice. Students should practice at home, too, involving family members if possible. As they rehearse, students should act like the character, reading the part the way the character would talk. Remind them to use their voices, faces, and bodies to show character's emotions. Each group should designate one person to tell the audience about the performance. (This information is included in the narrator's part in the scripts in the Appendix.) Performers may need to experiment to find comfortable positions that enable the audience to see their faces and hear their words clearly. Before the big day, decide on the order of performances and rehearse the program from start to finish to be sure everything will go smoothly.

*This narrator is ready to announce her group's performance of Cherry's* The Great Kapok Tree. *She will introduce the performance to the audience, show them the book, and present the performers and their roles. After the performance, she will thank the audience and lead performers in a bow.*

## During Performances

Students should hold their scripts at chest level so the audience can see their faces and hear their voices clearly. (Demonstrate by holding a script directly in front of your mouth to show students how difficult it is for others to hear.) Prepare students for unforeseen things that may crop up during the performance. For example, if someone in the group makes a mistake, they should ignore it and continue with the performance. If the audience's laughter is prolonged, students should pause briefly to be sure everyone can hear the next line. At the end of each performance, the narrator should thank the audience for its good attention, and ask the performers to take a bow. If there is another script to be performed, the narrator (or you) should ask the audience to quickly and quietly get ready to listen to the next performance.

*These students have chosen their favorite script, practiced and rehearsed all week, and are performing for an audience of parents, students, and teachers. They hold their scripts at chest level so the audience can see their faces and hear their voices clearly.*

## AUDIENCE MEMBERS

Brainstorm with students about what makes a good audience, including listening politely and showing appreciation to the performers. Refer to Box 5-3 for ideas. Allow for the possibility that some students may never have attended any kind of performance and, thus, may not know what to expect and how to behave. Some intermediate-grade students may be anxious or embarrassed about performing in front of friends from other classes. If students don't bring this up, mention it yourself and ask students to talk about what you can do to help them feel more comfortable. Potential problems can be avoided with advanced planning and honest, open talk of this kind. If possible, ask other teachers to discuss audience expectations with their classes before coming to the performance.

# Performance Day

Set up an area in the classroom with space for the performance and for the audience to sit on the floor. (Put chairs in back and reserve them for adults.) Give students time to rehearse their parts in the performance area. Set up the refreshments on a table in an area away from the performance area. Have a camera ready to take photos for the bulletin board.

*Providing a small snack, such as juice and cookies, helps to make a performance an even more exciting event for both the audience and performers.*

Greet audience members by thanking them for coming and explaining what Readers Theater is. Tell them that the performers have worked very hard, and that you know they will be a respectful audience. Show and explain the chart with "audience responsibilities" in Box 5-3. Then tell them to sit back and enjoy the performance.

Be ready to step in and remind the audience and performers of their responsibilities. If the program consists of a number of different performances, it's a good idea to have ready a few audience participation activities. For example, the audience could read a poem or sing together or everyone could stand up and do a quick stretch.

After the performance, thank the audience for their good attention. If you have refreshments, serve guests first, starting with families of students.

# Final Thought

It was a terrific first performance. The students did a great job, the audience laughed and cheered, and the parents were so proud of their children. You've already had several teachers ask you for copies of the scripts. Give yourself a pat on the back, congratulate your students for their hard work, and get ready for the next time.

# Closing Thoughts

As I read over this book, I realize that, through research, classroom visits, talking to educators, and just thinking, I have learned a great deal about Readers Theater that I didn't know before I started writing. I started out convinced that Readers Theater should be a part of every classroom; I'm even more convinced of that now. Readers Theater is not just a fun activity (although it definitely is fun). Readers Theater addresses reading fluency, comprehension, and interpretation, as well as every area of language arts. It's also a great addition to content areas. Unlike the traditional school play, Readers Theater involves all students in an interesting, engaging, motivating format and uses the materials that you have in your classroom. Readers Theater builds the confidence and skills of struggling readers, shy students, and second-language learners by matching them with appropriate materials and building in time for them to practice until they can read their parts fluently. Readers Theater reaches resistant readers in a way that few other approaches can.

Chances are you recognized your most challenging student or teaching situation in the examples in this book. Maybe you read about a script that you know your students will love. I hope this book has convinced you to try Readers Theater in your classroom and to incorporate new ideas and materials. You'll be glad you did.

# Appendix: Scripts

The scripts in this appendix are some of the "greatest hits" of my collection. I selected them to represent a range of styles and genres. Each can be used as a model for writing scripts based on similar books. (See the book lists in Chapter 4 for suggestions.) Be sure to use the book versions along with the scripts.

## General Tips on Adapting Scripts to Fit Your Situation

These scripts and others can be modified if needed for any size group. If you have a large group and few parts (for example, if you want your entire class to perform one Readers Theater script), students can share parts, reading chorally. You can also split roles to accommodate larger groups. (This works especially well in scripts with large narrator parts—for example, in *The Three Little Pigs: Nacho, Tito, and Miguel* and the stories from *Fox at School*.) Scripts with sound effects or repeated parts work well for students to read chorally. For example, a group of students could be assigned to read the part labeled "ALL" in *The Little Old Lady Who Was Not Afraid of Anything* and *The Librarian From the Black Lagoon*.

If students object to having a minor role (and most will, eventually), you can assign two or more roles to one student. This works best if the characters are not in the same scenes. For example, in *The Boy Who Cried Wolf*, the same group of students could play the fishermen, hunters, and townspeople. In *The Three Little Pigs: Nacho, Tito, and Miguel*, Mamá Pig only appears in the beginning of the story, while José the Wolf is only in later scenes, so the same student could play both roles. Similarly, in the script of "Fox on Stage," most of the action takes place at school. The character of Mom has only one line in a scene that takes place at Fox's home. The student who plays the teacher, Miss Moon, or one of Fox's school friends could also take the part of Mom. To signal the change in roles, the performer can use a simple prop or costume along with a tag board sign. Another option is to combine narrator parts if there is more than one (e.g., in *The Boy Who Cried Wolf* and *Shelia Rae, the Brave*) or the roles of minor characters (e.g., the kids in *The Librarian from the Black Lagoon*). Shepard's Web site offers some more tips on modifying stories or scripts for groups of various sizes or to make them more appropriate and entertaining for different audiences.

# Scripts Included

**Folk and Fairy Tales: Traditional Versions and Transformations or Variants**

*The Boy Who Cried Wolf*
(Freya Littledale, 1987) . . . . . . . . . . . . . . . . . . . . . . . . . . . . 79

*Los Tres Cerdos/The Three Little Pigs: Nacho, Tito, and Miguel*
(Bobbi Salinas, 1998). . . . . . . . . . . . . . . . . . . . . . . . . . . . . . . 82

**Funny Stories**

"Fox in Charge," "Fox Escapes," and "Fox on Stage" from
*Fox at School* (Edward Marshall, 1983) . . . . . . . . . . . . . . . . . 85

*The Librarian From the Black Lagoon* (Mike Thaler, 1997) . . . . . . . . . . 91

**Picture Books With Strong/Interesting Characters**

*Sheila Rae, the Brave* (Kevin Henkes, 1996) . . . . . . . . . . . . . . . . . . 94

**Cumulative Stories**

*The Little Old Lady Who Was Not Afraid of Anything*
(Linda Williams, 2002). . . . . . . . . . . . . . . . . . . . . . . . . . . . . . . 97

**Information Books**

"Mighty Mites" and "Billions of Bacteria" from *Micro Monsters:*
*Life Under the Microscope*
(Christopher Maynard, 1999) . . . . . . . . . . . . . . . . . . . . . . . . . 102

**Chapter Books/Novels**

"The Bet" from *How to Eat Fried Worms* (Rockwell, 1973). . . . . . . . . . 106

# The Boy Who Cried Wolf

## A Readers Theater Script Based on the Book by Freya Littledale

| CAST | Narrator 1 | Narrator 2 | Tom | Hunters |
|---|---|---|---|---|
| | Sheep | Fishermen | Wolf | Townspeople |

**Narrator 1:** [*Shows the book and reads the title and author. Introduces the cast.*]

**Narrator 2:** Once there was a shepherd boy called Tom. Day after day he sat on a hill and watched his sheep. Night after night, he went home, ate his supper, and fell asleep.

**Tom:** Nothing ever happens to me. I see hunters hunt in the woods and fishermen fish in the lake. But I just sit here and watch my sheep.

**Narrator 1:** And so he did. He watched the sheep eat the grass. He watched them sleep in the sun. He watched them follow the leader along the side of the hill.

**Narrator 2:** One morning Tom was watching his sheep when he saw some hunters walking through the woods and he decided to have some fun.

**Tom:** Help! Help! Help! A wolf is going to eat my sheep.

**Hunters:** Don't be afraid. We're coming.

**Narrator 1:** And they ran out of the woods with their great big guns.

**Hunters:** Where's the wolf?

**Tom:** Follow me.

**Narrator 2:** And he led the hunters down to the lake . . . and all around it.

**Tom:** He must have gone back to my sheep.

**Narrator 1:** And he led the hunters back to the sheep.

*Readers Theater for Building Fluency* ● Scholastic Teaching Resources

**Sheep:** Baaaa.

**Hunters:** There is no wolf!

**Tom:** You're right. There is no wolf. I fooled you!

**Narrator 2:** The hunters were very angry.

**Hunters:** You'll never fool us again!

**Narrator 1:** And off they went back into the woods.

**Narrator 2:** The next morning Tom was watching his sheep when he saw some fishermen down by the lake. He decided to have some more fun.

**Tom:** Help! Help! Help! A wolf is going to eat my sheep.

**Fishermen:** Don't worry. We'll help you.

**Narrator 1:** And they ran all the way up the hill.

**Fishermen:** Where's the wolf?

**Tom:** I saw him go into the woods. Follow me.

**Narrator 2:** And he led the fishermen into the woods . . . and out again.

**Sheep:** Baaaa.

**Fishermen:** There is no wolf.

**Tom:** Ha! Ha! Ha! You're right. There is no wolf. I fooled you!

**Narrator 1:** The fishermen were very angry.

**Fishermen:** We have better things to do than look for a wolf that isn't there.

**Narrator 2:** And they went back to the lake to catch some fish.

**Tom:** Oh, that was fun! I wish I could do it every day.

**Narrator 1:** The very next morning Tom was watching his sheep when he heard a horrible howl.

**Wolf:** Ah-whooooooo!

**Tom:** Who's there? Is it one of you men playing a trick on *me*?

**Narrator 2:** But no one answered. Then all at once Tom saw a great big wolf standing by his side.

**Wolf:** I like your sheep. I think I'll eat them for lunch.

**Tom:** You can't do that!

80

**Wolf:** Yes I can.

**Tom:** No you can't! I'm going to get help!

**Narrator 1:** And he ran all the way to town.

**Tom:** WOLF! WOLF! WOLF!

**Narrator 2:** The people of the town came running. The hunters and fishermen came, too.

**Tom:** A wolf is going to eat my sheep! Come with me!

**Hunters:** No! You fooled us before!

**Fishermen:** You fooled us, too!

**Townspeople:** We heard all about you. And you can't fool anyone here!

**Tom:** But I'm not fooling this time. I'm telling the truth. Follow me and you'll see.

**Hunters:** We don't believe you!

**Fishermen:** You tricked us!

**Townspeople:** Go back to your sheep!

**Tom:** Oh my! What can I do now?

**Narrator 1:** And he left the town and ran back up the hill.

**Narrator 2:** He looked and looked and looked. But he could not find a single sheep. The wolf had eaten them all.

**Tom:** Nobody came to help me. And now my sheep are gone.

**Wolf:** Heh! Heh! Heh! You told so many lies no one believed you when you told the truth!

**Narrator 1:** And away he went deep into the woods.

**Tom:** The wolf is right. I must tell the truth.

**ALL:** And from that time on, he always did.

# Los Tres Cerdos/The Three Little Pigs: Nacho, Tito, and Miguel

## A Readers Theater Script Based on the Book by Bobbi Salinas

**CAST**  Narrator  Mamá  Nacho
     Tito  Miguel  José (the wolf)

*Non-Speaking Parts:* cow, beaver, frog

**Narrator:** [*Shows the book and reads the title and author. Introduces the characters.*] Once upon a time there was a sow.

**Mamá:** Hello!

**Narrator:** She lived with her three piglets . . .

**Nacho:** Nacho . . .

**Tito:** Tito . . .

**Miguel:** . . . and Miguel. That's me.

**Narrator:** One day the pigs decided to take the money they had saved and leave home to seek new adventures and meet new friends.

**Mamá:** Be sure to come by for some homemade tortillas when you are in town.

**3 Pigs:** [together] Yes, *Mamá.*

**Mamá:** And ALWAYS watch out for José, the wolf.

**3 Pigs:** [together]. Yes, *Mamá.*

**Mamá:** *Adios.*

**3 Pigs:** *Adios.*

**Narrator:** The first pig, Nacho, found a nice place to build a house. Then he met a cow with some straw.

**Nacho:** May I buy some straw? I'd like to build a house with it.

**Narrator:** Nacho did buy the straw—and built his very own house.

**Nacho:** And a very nice straw house it was, too. It had a beautiful rug, a piano, and a ceiling fan.

**Narrator:** Just as Nacho lay down to read a book in his new house, along came the hungry wolf, José. The tricky wolf looked in the window.

**José:** Nacho, Nacho, let me come in.

**Nacho:** No way, José!
I won't let you come in—
Not by the hairs on my chinny-chin-chin.

**José:** Then I'll huff and I'll puff, and I'll blow your house in.

**Narrator:** So, he huffed and he puffed and blew the house in. Rug, piano, books, and all.

**Narrator:** José quickly tied Nacho up and threw him into an empty pigpen behind the house.

**Nacho:** Help!

**José:** M-m-m-m. This pig will make some delicious *carnitas* and *chicharrones* for supper tonight!

**Narrator:** The second pig, Tito, also found a nice place to build a house. Then he met a beaver with some wood.

**Tito:** May I buy some wood? I'd like to build a house with it.

**Narrator:** After he bought the wood, Tito built his very own wood house right underneath a deserted treehouse.

**Tito:** And a very nice house it was, too. Complete with my art work, my paints, and a porch swing.

**Narrator:** Just as Tito sat down to work on a painting in his new house, YOU KNOW WHO showed up outside.

**José:** Tito, Tito, let me come in.

**Tito:** No way, José!
I won't let you come in—
not by the hairs on my chinny-chin-chin.

**José:** Then I'll huff and I'll puff, and I'll blow your house in!

**Narrator:** So José huffed and he puffed, and he blew the house in. Art, paints, porch swing, and all. José quickly tied Tito up and threw him in the same pigpen he had thrown Nacho.

**Tito:** Help.

**José:** M-m-m-m. Another pig to eat. *Carnitas* and *chicharrones* for supper tomorrow night, too!

**Narrator:** The third pig, Miguel, also found a nice place to build a house. Then, he met a frog with some adobe bricks.

**Miguel:** May I buy some adobe bricks? I'd like to build a brick house with them.

**Narrator:** After he bought the adobe bricks, Miguel built his very own brick house.

**Miguel:** And a very nice house it was, too. Complete with pottery, a computer, and books.

**Narrator:** Just as Miguel sat down to work at this computer in his new house, YOU KNOW WHO peeked in the window.

**José:** Miguel, Miguel, let me come in.

**Miguel:** No way, José!
I won't let you come in—
Not by the hairs on my chinny-chin-chin.

**José:** Then I'll huff and I'll puff, and I'll blow your house in!

**Narrator:** So he huffed and he puffed, but nothing happened.
So he HUFFED and he PUFFED again,
and again, nothing happened.

**José:** [*panting*] Miguel, can't you hear me huffing and puffing out here?

**Narrator:** Miguel could see that José was beginning to fume from all the huffing and puffing.

Now José was mad enough to explode. He decided to play a trick on Miguel. Who do you think will win out in the end? Read the rest of the book to find out what happens.

Three Readers Theater Scripts
Based on the Book *Fox at School*
by Edward Marshall

# 1. "Fox in Charge"

**CAST**   Narrator      Carmen      Dexter      Fox
               Miss Moon   Principal   Class (3 or 4 students)

**Narrator:** [*Shows the book and introduces the characters.*] The title of this book is *Fox at School,* and it's written by Edward Marshall. The book has three stories about Fox and his friends. This story is called "Fox in Charge."

**Narrator:** Carmen, Dexter, and Fox were on their way to school.

**Carmen:** I'm going to be a pilot when I grow up.

**Dexter:** I think I'll be a cowboy.

**Carmen:** What about you, Fox?

**Fox:** I'm going to be a teacher.

**Carmen:** You're not serious.

**Fox:** It's an easy job.

**Narrator:** The next morning Fox was in for a big surprise.

**Miss Moon:** I must be away for a few minutes, and I'm putting Fox in charge.

**Fox:** Hot dog!

**Miss Moon:** Keep them under control.

**Fox:** Don't worry about a thing.

**Miss Moon:** You will mind Fox.

**Class:** Yes, Miss Moon.

**Miss Moon:** I'll be back.

**Narrator:** And she left the room.

**Fox:** Open your readers, please.

**Class:** You can't make us.

**Fox:** I'm in charge here. You will do as I say.

**Class:** That's what you think! We're going to have some fun!

**Narrator:** And in no time at all the room was a real zoo. Junior threw spitballs. Dexter stuck gum on Betty's tail. And Carmen showed everyone her underpants. The class was out of control. Fox looked out in the hall.

**Fox:** Here she comes!

**Narrator:** Everyone sat down—fast. They sat and waited for Miss Moon. She did not come.

**Dexter:** You tricked us! Now we're *really* going to go hog-wild.

**Narrator:** And they did. All of a sudden the principal stepped into the room. He was hopping mad!

**Principal:** What is the meaning of this?

**Dexter:** It's all Fox's fault! He's in charge.

**Principal:** Is that so, Dexter?

**Dexter:** He couldn't keep us under control.

**Principal:** I think someone should come with me to the office.

**Fox:** Uh-oh.

**Narrator:** When Miss Moon came back, she found the class all quiet.

**Miss Moon:** How nice. But where is Dexter?

**Class:** He's in the principal's office.

# 2. "Fox Escapes"

---

**CAST**  Narrator  Dexter  Carmen  Fox
Miss Moon  Junior  Principal

---

**Narrator:** [*Shows the book and introduces the characters.*] The title of this book is *Fox at School*, and it's written by Edward Marshall. The book has three stories about Fox and his friends at school. This story is called "Fox Escapes."

**Narrator:** [*Ringing a bell or shouting loudly*] DING! DING! DING!

**Dexter:** Fire drill!

**Carmen:** Oh, goody!

**Fox:** Oh, no.

**Miss Moon:** Now, single file.

**Carmen:** Fire drills are wild!

**Narrator:** The classroom was on the second floor, so the students had to climb out the window and slide down a slide to the ground. The class got out of the building in a hurry. Dexter sat on a piece of waxed paper to make himself go even faster.

**Carmen:** Whee!

**Miss Moon:** You're next, Fox.

**Narrator:** Fox looked down.

**Fox:** I don't care for this.

**Miss Moon:** Go on, Fox.

**Narrator:** But Fox didn't move.

**Junior/
Carmen/Dexter:** Come on, Fox!

**Junior:** It's fun!

**Carmen:** It's wild!

**Dexter:** Fox is scared!

**Miss Moon:** You're not afraid, are you, Fox?

**Fox:** Yes.

**Miss Moon:** There's nothing to be afraid of. It's easy as pie.

**Fox:** You may go first.

**Miss Moon:** Not on your life! *I* always take the stairs.

**Fox:** You aren't afraid, are you?

**Miss Moon:** Uh.

**Principal:** Who is holding up this fire drill?

**Dexter:** It's Fox.

**Principal:** Come down this minute. And you, too, Miss Moon.

**Fox:** I'll go first.

**Narrator:** He closed his eyes. And down he went.

**Fox:** It's as easy as pie!

**Narrator:** Miss Moon took a deep breath. And down she went.

**ALL:** We're very proud of you, Miss Moon!

# 3. "Fox on Stage"

| CAST | Narrator | Miss Moon | Carmen | Junior |
|------|----------|-----------|--------|--------|
|      | Fox      | Dexter    | Louise | Mom    |

**Narrator:** [*Shows the book and introduces the characters.*] The title of this book is *Fox at School*, and it's written by Edward Marshall. The book has three stories about Fox and his friends at school. This story is called "Fox on Stage."

**Narrator:** Fox wanted a part in the class play.

**Miss Moon:** We must be fair. I'll put everyone's name in a shoe box. Now, let's see who will play the pretty princess.

**Narrator:** She drew out the first name.

88

**Miss Moon:** The pretty princess will be played by Carmen.

**Carmen:** O, goody!

**Miss Moon:** And now for the part of the mean dragon.

**Narrator:** Fox held his breath.

**Miss Moon:** The mean dragon will be played by Junior.

**Junior:** I'll do my best.

**Miss Moon:** And now for the part of the handsome prince.

**Narrator:** Fox bit his nails.

**Miss Moon:** That part goes to Fox.

**Fox:** Hot dog!

**Dexter:** Rats.

**Miss Moon:** Everyone else will play flowers and trees.

**Fox:** Gosh. The handsome prince.

**Miss Moon:** Now, now. It is a hard part. You must learn it by heart.

**Fox:** Don't worry.

**Narrator:** That night Fox could not sleep. He was thinking about the play.

**Fox:** I'll be great! The girls will follow me around!

**Narrator:** The next morning Fox went down to eat breakfast with his sister, Louise, and his mother. [*Fox is wearing a paper crown and sunglasses.*]

**Louise:** Mom, Fox is acting funny.

**Mom:** So I see.

**Fox:** You may bow.

**Louise:** Do you know your part?

**Fox:** There's nothing to it.

**Narrator:** At recess that day, Junior and Carmen worked on their parts.

**Junior:** Come on, Fox. Let's practice.

**Narrator:** But Fox was busy talking to a group of girls.

**Fox:** I will be a big hit.

**Narrator:** The next day at play practice Carmen and Junior were very nervous.

**Carmen:** I may throw up.

**Fox:** Calm down.

**Miss Moon:** Is everybody ready? Curtain going up!

**Narrator:** Carmen, the princess, and Junior, the mean dragon, were on stage.

**Carmen:** Here I am, all alone in the forest.

**Junior:** Ah-ha! I am going to eat you up!

**Carmen:** Help! Help! Who will save me?

**Narrator:** Everyone looked at Fox. But Fox just stood there.

**Carmen:** Who will save me?

**Narrator:** And everyone looked at Fox.

**Fox:** Uh.

**Narrator:** Miss Moon was very cross.

**Miss Moon:** You did not study your part! You are not serious about this play.

**Dexter:** Miss Moon, Miss Moon. I know the part of the handsome prince. And I know it by heart!

**Miss Moon:** Really Dexter?

**Narrator:** The night of the play everyone was excited.

**Carmen:** I hope I don't throw up.

**Junior:** I hope I don't forget my lines.

**Narrator:** But no one forgot. Carmen was very pretty as the princess. Junior made a fine dragon. Dexter was very good as the handsome prince. And Fox . . .

**Louise:** You were the best tree in the whole play.

**Fox:** Just wait until next year.

### Special Directions:

*Note that "Mom" has only one line. Her part can be played by the teacher or another character who is not in the same scene (e.g., Miss Moon, Carmen, Junior, or Dexter). Be sure to distinguish the characters by giving "Mom" a special prop.*

# The Librarian From the Black Lagoon

## A Readers Theater Script Based on the Book by Mike Thaler

**CAST**   Kid 1   Kid 2   **Mrs. Beamster**
Kid 3   Kid 4

**Kid 4:** [*Shows the book and reads the title and author. Introduces the characters.*] This story is about some kids who are visiting the school library for the first time.

**Kid 1:** Today our class is going to the library. We've been hearing some scary things about the place.

**Kid 2:** The library is somewhere behind the boiler room. It's called . . .

**ALL:** MEDIA CENTER OF THE EARTH

**Kid 3:** Mrs. Beamster is the librarian. The kids call her . . .

**ALL:** THE LAMINATOR.

**Kid 4:** They say she laminates you if you talk in the library.

**Kid 1:** She also has a library assistant named . . .

**ALL:** IGOR.

**Kid 2:** You know you're getting close to the library by the signs on the wall.

**ALL:** [*Point to signs and read*]
NO TALKING BEYOND THIS POINT.
NO WHISPERING BEYOND THIS POINT.
NO BREATHING BEYOND THIS POINT.

**Kid 3:** They say you're allowed to stay in the library as long as you can hold your breath.

**Kid 4:** Some kids last as long as a minute. That doesn't include time in the . . .

**ALL:** DECONTAMINATION ROOM.

**Kid 1:** There you put on hair nets and rubber gloves. Next, you have to go through the . . .

**ALL:** GUM DETECTOR.

**Kid 2:** Once you're finally in the library, you can't actually check out books.

**Kid 3:** In fact, you can't take them off the shelves. Mrs. Beamster bolts them together.

**Kid 4:** Also, they say, the shelves are electrified.

**Kid 1:** If you twist your neck and squint, you can read the spines.

**Kid 2:** Everyone says the best part of a library visit is . . .

**ALL:** STORYTIME

**Kid 3:** All the kids stand at attention while Mrs. Beamster reads one of the cards from the card catalogue.

**Kid 4:** Or, if you catch her in a good mood, she'll recite the Dewey decimal system by heart.

**Kid 1:** They say Mrs. Beamster has a crush on Mr. Dewey and that she carries his picture in a lead locket around her neck.

**Kid 2:** She also has rubber stamps on the soles of her shoes. And, wherever she steps . . . it says . . .

**ALL:** OVERDUE!

**Kid 3:** She seems to have ears on the back of her head. If she catches you whispering . . .

**ALL:** YOU'RE LAMINATED!

**Kid 4:** They say she puts glue on all the chairs so you won't WRIGGLE.

**Kid 1:** Then she shows you slides of all her vacations since 1902. She goes to the same place every year—the Library of Congress.

**Kid 2:** Mrs. Beamster also subscribes to three magazines.

**Kid 3:** *The Morticians Monthly, The Complete Pamphlet of Zip Codes,* and *Spots Illustrated: The Magazine for Cleaner Laundry.* These you DO get to read.

**Kid 4:** But stay away from her plants. They are VENUS FLY TRAPS!

**Kid 1:** And don't pet the animals in her petting zoo, which contains a PIRANHA and a PORCUPINE.

**Kid 2:** Don't go near her computer either. It uses a real MOUSE!

**Kid 3:** Well, it's time to go. As we get near the library there are lots of signs.

**ALL:** [*Point to signs and read*]
BOOKS ARE FUN! BOOKS ARE JOY! READ! WE SPRAY FOR BOOKWORMS! BOOKS CAN TAKE YOU EVERYWHERE! WELCOME.

**Kid 4:** We march right in and sit down in little chairs. These must be the ones without glue.

**Kid 1:** Mrs. Beamster comes over with an armful of books and puts them on our table.

**Mrs. Beamster:** Hello children. Welcome to the library.

**Kid 2:** Then she smiles and hands me one. It's a book of KNOCK-KNOCK JOKES!

**Mrs. Beamster:** I saved this one for you.

**Kid 3:** [*Pretending to read from the joke book*] Knock-Knock.

**Kid 4:** Who's there?

**Kid 3:** Dishes.

**Kid 4:** Dishes who?

**Kid 3:** Dishes a nice place to be.

**ALL:** I'M GOING TO LOVE THE LIBRARY.

*Special Directions:*

*You will need these props:*

1. *A book of knock-knock jokes (or you can cover a book with paper and write "Knock-Knock Jokes" on the cover).*

2. *Large signs with the words below. Hang them on a wall near the performance area.*

   NO TALKING BEYOND THIS POINT.
   NO WHISPERING BEYOND THIS POINT.
   NO BREATHING BEYOND THIS POINT.

3. *Make large signs with the words below and hang them on the wall.*
   *Keep them covered until the cast is ready to read them.*

   | | |
   |---|---|
   | BOOKS ARE FUN! | BOOKS ARE JOY! |
   | READ! | WE SPRAY FOR BOOKWORMS! |
   | WELCOME! | BOOKS CAN TAKE YOU EVERYWHERE! |

# Sheila Rae, the Brave

## A Readers Theater Script Based on the Book by Kevin Henkes

*Script Written by Jason Buckingham*

**CAST**    Narrator 1    Narrator 2    Sheila Rae    Louise

**Narrator 1:** [*Shows the book and reads the title and author. Introduces the characters.*] This is Sheila Rae. She's not afraid of anything.

**Narrator 2:** She's not afraid of the dark or thunder and lightning.

**Sheila Rae:** I'm not even afraid of the big black dog at the end of the block.

**Narrator 1:** At dinner Sheila Rae makes believe that the cherries in her fruit cocktail are the eyes of dead bears.

**Sheila Rae:** I can eat five eyes at once!

**Narrator 2:** At school Sheila Rae giggles when the principal walks by. And when her classmate Wendell stole her jump rope during recess, Sheila Rae tied him up until the bell rang.

**Sheila Rae:** I am very brave.

**Narrator 1:** Sheila Rae steps on every crack in the sidewalk without fear. When her sister Louise said there was a monster in the closet, Sheila Rae attacked it.

**Narrator 2:** And she rode her bicycle no-handed with her eyes closed. Her friends would cheer.

**ALL:** Yea, Yea, Sheila Rae!

**Narrator 1:** One day Sheila Rae decided to walk home from school a new way but Louise was afraid to.

**Louise:** You're too brave for me.

**Sheila Rae:** You're always such a scaredy cat.

**Louise:** Am not.

**Narrator 1:** Sheila Rae started off skipping and singing.

**Sheila Rae:** I am brave. I am fearless.

**Narrator 2:** She stepped on every crack. She walked backward with her eyes closed. And she pretended that the trees were evil creatures.

**Sheila Rae:** So I climbed up and broke their fingers off.

**ALL:** SNAP! SNAP! SNAP!

**Narrator 1:** Sheila Rae walked and walked. She turned corners. She crossed streets.

**Narrator 2:** It suddenly occurred to Sheila Rae that nothing looked familiar. Sheila Rae heard frightening noises.

**Sheila Rae:** They sounded worse than thunder.

**Narrator 1:** She thought terrible thoughts worse than anything she had ever imagined. She tried to convince herself she was brave.

**Sheila Rae:** I am brave. I am fearless.

**Narrator 2:** The sounds became more frightening. The thoughts became more horrible. Sheila Rae sat down on a rock and cried.

**Sheila Rae:** Help! Mother, Father, Louise!

**Narrator 1:** Suddenly, Louise swung down from the tree above.

**Louise:** Here I am.

**Sheila Rae:** Louise!

**Narrator 2:** Sheila Rae hugged her sister.

**Sheila Rae:** We're lost.

**Louise:** No we're not. I know the way home. Follow me!

**Narrator 1:** Louise stepped on every crack. She walked backward with her eyes closed.

**Narrator 2:** She growled at the stray dogs and bared her teeth at stray cats. And she pretended that the trees were evil creatures.

**Louise:** I jumped up and broke their fingers off.

**ALL:** SNAP! SNAP! SNAP!

**Narrator 1:** Sheila Rae walked quietly behind her sister until their house was in sight.

**Narrator 2:** When they reached their own yard and the gate was closed behind them Sheila Rae hugged her sister again.

**Sheila Rae:** Louise, you are brave. You are fearless.

**Louise:** We both are!

**Narrator 1:** And they walked backward into the house. With their eyes closed.

# The Little Old Lady Who Was Not Afraid of Anything

## A Readers Theater Script Based on the Book by Linda Williams

**CAST**  Narrator 1     Narrator 2     Narrator 3

Narrator 4     Little Old Lady     6 sign holders

**Narrator 1:** [*Shows the book and reads the title and author. Introduces the cast. Invites the audience to stand up for the performance. Asks them to read the signs and do the actions.*]

**Narrator 1:** Once upon a time, there was a little old lady who was not afraid of anything!

**Narrator 2:** One windy afternoon the little old lady left her cottage and went for a walk in the forest to collect herbs and spices, nuts and seeds.

**Narrator 3:** She walked so long and so far that it started to get dark. There was only a sliver of moon shining through the night. The little old lady started to walk home.

**Narrator 4:** Suddenly she stopped! Right in the middle of the path were two big shoes. And the shoes went . . .

**ALL:** CLOMP, CLOMP.

**Little Old Lady:** Get out of my way, you two big shoes! I'm not afraid of you!

**Narrator 1:** On she walked down the path. But behind her she could hear two shoes go . . .

**ALL:** CLOMP, CLOMP.

**Narrator 2:** A little farther on, the little old lady stumbled into a pair of pants. And the pants went . . .

**ALL:** WIGGLE, WIGGLE.

**Little Old Lady:** Get out of my way, you pair of pants. I'm not afraid of you!

**Narrator 3:** And the little old lady walked on. But behind her she could hear two shoes go . . .

**ALL:** CLOMP, CLOMP.

**Narrator 3:** And one pair of pants go . . .

**ALL:** WIGGLE, WIGGLE.

**Narrator 4:** Farther still, the little old lady bumped into a shirt. And the shirt went . . .

**ALL:** SHAKE, SHAKE.

**Little Old Lady:** Get out of my way, you silly shirt. I'm not afraid of you!

**Narrator 4:** And the little lady walked on a little bit faster. But behind her she could hear two shoes go . . .

**ALL:** CLOMP, CLOMP.

**Narrator 4:** One pair of pants go . . .

**ALL:** WIGGLE, WIGGLE.

**Narrator 4:** And one shirt go . . .

**ALL:** SHAKE, SHAKE.

**Narrator 1:** A little ways on, the little old lady came upon two white gloves and a tall black hat. And the gloves went . . .

**ALL:** CLAP, CLAP.

**Narrator 1:** And the hat went . . .

**ALL:** NOD, NOD.

**Little Old Lady:** Get out of my way, you two white gloves and you tall black hat! I'm not afraid of you!

**Narrator 2:** And the little lady walked on, just a little bit faster. But behind her she could hear two shoes go . . .

**ALL:** CLOMP, CLOMP.

**Narrator 2:** One pair of pants go . . .

**ALL:** WIGGLE, WIGGLE.

**Narrator 2:** One shirt go . . .

**ALL:** SHAKE, SHAKE.

**Narrator 2:** Two gloves go . . .

**ALL:** CLAP, CLAP.

**Narrator 2:** And one hat go . . .

**ALL:** NOD, NOD.

**Narrator 3:** By now the little old lady was walking at quite a fast pace. She was very near her cottage when she was startled by a very huge, very orange, very scary pumpkin head. And the head went . . .

**ALL:** BOO! BOO!

**Narrator 4:** This time the little old lady did not stop to talk. She did not stop at all. She ran! But behind her she could hear two shoes go . . .

**ALL:** CLOMP, CLOMP.

**Narrator 4:** One pair of pants go . . .

**ALL:** WIGGLE, WIGGLE.

**Narrator 4:** One shirt go . . .

**ALL:** SHAKE, SHAKE.

**Narrator 4:** Two gloves go . . .

**ALL:** CLAP, CLAP.

**Narrator 4:** One hat go . . .

**ALL:** NOD, NOD.

**Narrator 4:** And one scary pumpkin head go . . .

**ALL:** BOO! BOO!

**Narrator 1:** The little old lady did not look back. She ran as fast as she could and didn't stop to catch her breath until she was safe inside her cottage with the door locked. She sat in her chair by the fire and she rocked and she rocked. Until she heard a knock.

**ALL:** KNOCK, KNOCK.

**Little Old Lady:** I wonder who could be knocking on the door? Should I answer it? Well, I am not afraid of anything!

**Narrator 2:** So she went to the door and opened it. What do you think she saw? Two shoes go . . .

**ALL:** CLOMP, CLOMP.

**Narrator 3:** One pair of pants go . . .

**ALL:** WIGGLE, WIGGLE.

**Narrator 4:** One shirt go . . .

**ALL:** SHAKE, SHAKE.

**Narrator 1:** Two gloves go . . .

**ALL:** CLAP, CLAP.

**Narrator 2:** One hat go . . .

**ALL:** NOD, NOD.

**Narrator 3:** And one scary pumpkin head go . . .

**ALL:** BOO! BOO!

**Little Old Lady:** I'm not afraid of you. What do you want anyway?

**ALL:** WE'VE COME TO SCARE YOU!

**Little Old Lady:** You can't scare me!

**Narrator 4:** The pumpkin head suddenly looked very unhappy.

**ALL:** What's to become of us?

**Little Old Lady:** I have an idea!

**Narrator 1:** She whispered into the pumpkin's ear. The pumpkin head nodded and its face seemed to brighten.

**Little Old Lady:** Goodnight!

**Narrator 2:** The next morning she woke up early. She went to her window and looked out into her garden. And what do you think she saw? Two shoes go . . .

**ALL:** CLOMP, CLOMP.

**Narrator 3:** One pair of pants go . . .

**ALL:** WIGGLE, WIGGLE.

**Narrator 4:** One shirt go . . .

**ALL:** SHAKE, SHAKE.

**Narrator 1:** Two gloves go . . .

**ALL:** CLAP, CLAP.

**Narrator 2:** One hat go . . .

**ALL:** NOD, NOD.

**Narrator 3:** One scary pumpkin head go . . .

**ALL:** BOO! BOO!

**Narrator 4:** Together they formed the perfect scarecrow.

**Little Old Lady:** And frightened all the birds away!

## Stage notes:

*For the six sign holders, make large signs for each of the sounds (below). Invite the audience to stand up during the performance and to join in, reading the signs and performing the actions, when the signs are held up. All of the actors can make the actions with the audience.*

CLOMP, CLOMP

WIGGLE, WIGGLE

SHAKE, SHAKE

CLAP, CLAP

NOD, NOD

BOO! BOO!

# Two Readers Theater Scripts Based on the Book
*Micro Monsters: Life Under the Microscope*
by Christopher Maynard

# 1. "Mighty Mites"

*Script Written by Gay Ivey*

**CAST**  Narrator 1    Chorus (or all actors)    Dust Mite 1
            Dust Mite 2    Eyelash Mite              Itch Mite

**Narrator:** [*Shows the book and reads the title and author. Introduces the characters.*]

**Chorus:** Did you know that more than a million eight-legged, hump-backed creatures are probably living under your bed?

**Dust Mites:** We are dust mites—and I'll bet lots of us live all over your home. Any place that is humid and warm suits us just fine.

**Narrator:** Dust mites mostly live in dust, especially in places that trap tufts of it—like deep carpets, pillows, bedding, and sofas. Dust might seem like a strange place to live.

**Chorus:** But it isn't if you look at it closely.

**Narrator:** Dust is mostly made up of strands of hair, clothes, fibers, carpet fluff, and countless flakes of human skin.

**Dust Mite 1:** And skin flakes are we what mites really love to eat. It's why so many of us crowd together in mattresses and in carpets under beds.

**Dust Mite 2:** For us, these places are just like orchards where millions of delicious skin flakes drop from human beings every day. We have no jaws and we can't chew our food.

**Dust Mites:** Instead, we belch digestive juices onto our food to turn it into liquid. Then we suck it up, just like milkshake through a straw.

**Itch Mite:** I am a female itch mite.

**Chorus:** A cousin of the dust mites.

**Itch Mite:** Instead of eating skin flakes, we itch mites burrow right into human skin!

**Narrator:** The good news is that the male itch mites stay on the surface and do little harm.

**Chorus:** The bad news is that the females are great diggers and can spread from person to person like wildfire.

**Itch Mite:** We use our mouth and front legs to bite into skin cells and suck out the fluid inside. We don't go deeper than the outer layers of skin.

**Chorus:** That's why no blood comes gushing out.

**Itch Mite:** But our burrows can wind along for over an inch.

**Narrator:** A burrow isn't much wider than a hair, so it's nearly impossible for humans to see.

**Itch Mite:** But they can't miss the itchy rash we give them! As we dig, we lay eggs, usually about three a day. After eight weeks and over 150 eggs, we die.

**Narrator:** Within three or four days the eggs hatch out and baby mites climb to the surface, where they live until they start to lay eggs themselves.

**Eyelash Mite:** I am an eyelash mite. Imagine being as small as me and living on a great, big, blinking eyelash. Whenever the eyelids flutter, I go up and down, up and down.

**Chorus:** It's like living on a giant merry-go-round.

**Eyelash Mite:** We eyelash mites are really small—much smaller than our itch mite cousins—and we are colorless, too.

**Narrator:** So if you haven't got a very powerful microscope, don't even try to look for them. It's impossible.

**Eyelash Mite:** But if you did look at us through a microscope, you would see a cigar-shaped body and four pairs of legs.

**Chorus:** These are the only features that give them away.

**Eyelash Mite:** For most of our lives, we live harmlessly in the socket, or follicle, of an eyelash. We hang on to the lash, a bit like a caterpillar hangs on to a tree, but always pointing head down so we can suck up the juices that ooze out of human skin.

**Narrator:** Because they don't burrow into skin, eyelash mites don't have any serious ill effects on people.

**Eyelash Mite:** And because we are invisible, nobody really takes much notice of us at all.

**Chorus:** To learn more about other tiny creatures, read *Micro Monsters: Life Under the Microscope* by Christopher Maynard.

# 2. "Billions of Bacteria"

| CAST | Narrator 1 | Narrator 2 | E. coli |
|------|-----------|-----------|---------|
| | Soil Bacteria | Streptococcus (Strep) | |

**Narrator 1:** [*Shows the book and reads the title and author. Introduces the characters.*]

**Narrator 2:** You cough. You moan. Your throat feels raw, like a razor is cutting into it.

**All Bacteria:** You've caught a bug and . . . that's where we come in. We're bacteria, the smallest form of life on earth

**Strep:** I am a streptococcus bacteria. You can call me strep. I'm so small, I'm invisible, but I pack a terrific wallop if I infect someone's throat. Once I get in, I multiply like crazy in the wet warmth.

**Narrator 1:** By the end of just one day, there may be hundreds of millions of bacteria lining the walls of the throat.

**Strep:** Humans react violently to me and my kin.

**Narrator 1:** They come down with a painful illness known as strep throat. The inside of the gullet turns an angry red color. It becomes dotted with specks of pus.

**Narrator 2:** Glands in the neck become tender. Soon swallowing hurts so badly it is almost impossible to eat. Fever, chills, headaches, and stomach aches pile on the misery.

**All Bacteria:** Even with medical attention, people stay sick anywhere from three to five days.

**Strep:** Fortunately, I am a mild bacteria. It is easy to get rid of me using antibiotics—drugs that help the human body fight off bacteria.

**All Bacteria:** But some of us are real thugs and can do nasty things to humans.

**E. coli:** I'm E. coli. I live in animal intestines. There, I stop other harmful bacteria from growing and help to make important vitamins.

**Narrator 1:** But one rare strain of the family is a brute. It can wreck the lining of the intestine and cause terrible cramps, diarrhea, and vomiting.

**Narrator 2:** It is mostly picked up by people who have eaten undercooked infected meat.

**All Bacteria:** But please don't get us wrong. Not all of us bacteria are bad guys. Some of us do a lot of good.

**Narrator 1:** For example, soil is packed with all kinds of bacteria.

**Soil Bacteria:** Like me. Many of us spend our time recycling animal dung or making sure dead creatures and plants rot. We can help to keep a field of cows healthy by working with dung beetles to break down the cow's dung and turning it into mulch to enrich the soil.

**All Bacteria:** If we bacteria didn't do our stuff, dead plants and animals would litter the landscape forever.

**Narrator 2:** To learn more about other tiny creatures, read *Micro Monsters: Life Under the Microscope* by Christopher Maynard.

# "The Bet" *from* How to Eat Fried Worms

## A Readers Theater Script Based on the Book by Thomas Rockwell

**CAST**    Narrator    Alan    Billy    Tom

**Narrator:** [*Shows the book and introduces the characters.*] The title of this book is *How to Eat Fried Worms* and it's written by Thomas Rockwell. This book is about three boys who make a disgusting bet. This Readers Theater is from the first chapter, which is called, "The Bet." When the story opens, Billy and Alan are talking to Tom about what they did the night before.

**Alan:** Hey Tom, where were you last night?

**Billy:** Yeah, you missed it.

**Alan:** What happened?

**Tom:** My mother kept me in.

**Alan:** What for?

**Tom:** I wouldn't eat my dinner.

**Alan:** What was it?

**Tom:** Salmon casserole.

**Billy:** That's not that bad

**Alan:** Yeah. Wouldn't she let you just eat two bites? Sometimes my mother says, well, all right, if I'll just eat two bites.

**Tom:** I wouldn't eat even one.

**Billy:** That's stupid. One bite can't hurt you. I'd eat one bite of anything before I'd let them send me up to my room right after supper.

**Narrator:** Tom shrugged. Alan thought a minute and then turned to Billy.

106

**Alan:** How about mud? You wouldn't eat a bite of mud.

**Billy:** Sure I would. Mud. What's mud? Just dirt with a little water in it. My father says everyone eats a pound of dirt every year anyway.

**Alan:** How about poison?

**Billy:** That's different.

**Alan:** How about worms?

**Billy:** Sure. Why not? Worms are just dirt.

**Alan:** Yeah, but they bleed.

**Billy:** So you'd have to cook them. Cows bleed.

**Tom:** I bet a hundred dollars you wouldn't really eat a worm. You talk big now, but you wouldn't if you were sitting at the dinner table with a worm on your plate.

**Billy:** I bet I would. I'd eat *fifteen* worms if somebody'd bet me a hundred dollars.

**Alan:** You *really* want to bet? *I'll* bet you fifty dollars you can't eat fifteen worms. I really will.

**Billy:** Where are you going to get fifty dollars?

**Alan:** In my savings account. I've got one hundred and thirty dollars and seventy-nine cents in my savings account. I know, because last week I put in the five dollars my grandmother gave me for my birthday.

**Billy:** Your mother wouldn't let you take it out.

**Alan:** She would if I lost the bet. I earned the money mowing lawns, so I can do whatever I want with it. I'll bet you fifty dollars you can't eat fifteen worms. Come on. You're chicken. You know you can't do it.

**Tom:** *I* wouldn't do it. If salmon casserole makes me sick, think what fifteen worms would do.

**Billy:** What type of worms?

**Alan:** Regular worms.

**Billy:** Not those big green ones that get on tomatoes. I won't eat those. And I won't eat them all at once. It might make me sick. One worm a day for fifteen days.

**Tom:** And he can eat them any way he wants. Boiled, stewed, fried, fricasseed.

**Narrator:** Billy thought about it. Fifty dollars was a lot of money. How bad could a worm taste? He'd eaten fried liver, mushrooms, pig's feet. All kinds of nasty stuff. And if he won the fifty dollars, he could buy that minibike he wanted. Heck, he could gag *anything* down for fifty dollars, couldn't he? He looked up.

**Billy:** I can use ketchup or mustard or anything like that? As much as I want?

**Alan:** Sure, anything. Okay?

**Billy:** Okay. I'll do it.

**Narrator:** If you want to find out what happens in the rest of the book, read *How to Eat Fried Worms.*

# Professional References Cited

Aaron, P. G. *Dyslexia and Hyperlexia: Diagnosis and Management of Developmental Reading Disabilities*. Dordrecht, Netherlands: Kluwer Academic Publishers, 1989.

Adams, M. J. *Beginning to Read: Thinking and Learning about Print*. Cambridge, MA: MIT Press, 1990.

Carver, R., & Hoffman, J. "The Effect of Practice Through Repeated Reading on Gain in Reading Ability Using a Computer-Based Instructional System." *Reading Research Quarterly,* 16, (1981): 374–390.

Chomsky, C. "When You Still Can't Read in Third Grade: After Decoding, What?" In S. J. Samuels (Ed.), *What Research Has to Say about Reading Instruction* (pp. 13–30). Newark, DE: International Reading Association, 1978.

Cunningham, P., & Allington, R. *Classrooms That Work: They Can All Read and Write* (3rd ed.). Boston: Allyn & Bacon, 2003.

Dowhower, S. L. "Speaking of Prosody: Fluency's Unattended Bedfellow." *Theory into Practice,* 30 (1991): 165–175.

Elley, W. "The Potential of Book Floods for Raising Literacy Levels." *International Review of Education,* 46 (2000): 233–255.

Graves, M. F., Juel, C., & Graves, B. B. *Teaching Reading in the 21st Century* (3rd ed.). Boston: Allyn & Bacon, 2004.

Hanson-Harding, A. *Great American Speeches, Grades 4–8*. New York: Scholastic, 1999.

Holdaway, D. *Foundations of Literacy*. Sydney, Australia: Ashton Scholastic, 1979.

Ivey, G., & Broaddus, K. "Just Plain Reading: A Survey of What Makes Middle School Students Want to Read." *Reading Research Quarterly,* 36 (2001): 350–377.

Mackey, M. "Filling the Gaps: The Baby-Sitters Club, the Series Books, and the Learning Reader." *Language Arts,* 67 (1990): 484–489.

Matzke, H. A., & Foltz, F. M. *Synopsis of Neuroanatomy* (4th ed.). New York: Oxford University Press, 1983.

Measley, D. "Understanding the Motivational Problems of At-Risk College Students." *Journal of Reading,* 33 (1990): 593–601.

National Reading Panel. *Teaching Children to Read: An Evidence-Based Assessment of Scientific Research Literature on Reading and its Implications for Reading Instruction*. Bethesda, MD: National Institutes of Health, 2000.

Neuman, S. "Books Make a Difference: A Study of Access to Literacy." *Reading Research Quarterly,* 34 (1999): 286–311.

Pearson, P. D., & Gallagher, M. C. "The Instruction of Reading Comprehension." *Contemporary Educational Psychology,* 8 (1983): 317–344.

Prescott, J. O. "The Power of Reader's Theater." *Instructor,* 22–24, Jan-Feb. (2003): 26, 82–84.

Rasinski, T. *The Fluent Reader: Oral Reading Strategies for Building Word Recognition, Fluency, and Comprehension.* New York: Scholastic, 2003.

Rinehart, S. D. "Don't Think for a Minute That I'm Getting Up There: Opportunities for Readers' Theater in a Tutorial for Children with Reading Problems." *Journal of Reading Psychology,* 20 (1999): 71–89.

Samuels, S. J. "Toward a Theory of Automatic Information Processing in Reading, Revisited." In R. Ruddell & N. J. Unrau (Eds.), *Theoretical Models and Processes of Reading* (4th ed.). Newark, DE: International Reading Association, 2004.

Sebesta, S. *The Art of Teaching.* Retrieved from www.teachervision.com/tv/resources/specialist/ssebesta2.html. July 7, 2003.

Shepard, A. *Aaron Shepard's RT Page.* Retrieved from www.aaronshep.com/rt, July 7, 2003.

Strecker, S. K., Roser, N. L., & Martinez, M. G. "Toward Understanding Oral Reading Fluency." *Yearbook of the National Reading Conference,* 48 (1999): 295–310.

Tyler, B. & Chard, D. J. "Using Readers' Theater to Foster Fluency in Struggling Readers: A Twist on the Repeated Reading Strategy." *Reading and Writing Quarterly,* 16 (2000): 163–168.

Walker, L. *Scripts for Schools.* Retrieved from www.scriptsforschools.com/1.html, July 7, 2003.

Wolf, S. "What's in a Name? Labels and Literacy in Readers Theater." *The Reading Teacher,* 46 (1993): 540–545.

Wolf, S. "The Flight of Reading: Shifts in Instruction, Orchestration, and Attitudes Through Classroom Theatre." *Reading Research Quarterly,* 33 (1998): 382–415.

Worthy, J. "A Matter of Interest: Literature That Hooks Reluctant Readers and Keeps Them Reading." *The Reading Teacher,* 50 (1996): 204–212.

Worthy, J., & Broaddus, K. "Fluency Beyond the Primary Grades: From Group Performance To Silent, Independent Reading." *The Reading Teacher,* 55 (2001/2002): 334–343.

Worthy, J., Broaddus, K., & Ivey, G. *Pathways to Independence: Reading, Writing, and Learning in Grades 3–8.* New York: The Guilford Press, 2001.

Worthy, J., & Invernizzi, M. "Linking Reading with Meaning: A Case Study of a Hyperlexic Reader." *JRB (Journal of Reading Behavior): A Journal of Literacy,* 27 (1996): 585–603.

# Selected Children's Books Cited

Allard, H. *Miss Nelson is Missing*. Boston: Houghton Mifflin, 1985.

Avi. *Nothing But the Truth*. New York: Avon, 1993.

Avi. *The True Confessions of Charlotte Doyle*. New York: Orchard, 1990.

Blume, J. *Freckle Juice*. New York: Yearling, 1978.

Brown, M. *Arthur's Birthday*. Boston: Little, Brown, 1991.

Brown, M. *Arthur's Teacher Trouble*. Boston: Little, Brown, 1989.

Browne, A. *Voices in the Park*. New York: Dorling Kindersley, 1998.

Cherry, L. *The Great Kapok Tree*. New York: Gulliver Green, 1990.

Cronin, D. *Click, Clack, Moo: Cows That Type*. New York: Simon & Schuster, 2000.

Curtis, C. *The Watsons Go to Birmingham—1963*. New York: Delacorte Books for Young Readers, 1995.

Danziger, P. *Amber Brown is not a Crayon*. New York: Putnam, 1995.

DiCamillo, K. *Because of Winn-Dixie*. New York: Candlewick Press, 2001.

Fletcher, R. *Flying Solo*. New York: Clarion, 1998.

Fox, M. *Hattie and the Fox*. New York: Simon & Schuster, 1992.

Galdone, P. *The Little Red Hen*. Boston: Houghton Mifflin, 1998.

Hayes, J. *La Llorona/The Weeping Woman*. Houston, TX: Cinco Puntos Press, 1990.

Hayes, J. *Estrellita de Oro: A Cinderella Cuento*. Houston, TX: Cinco Puntos Press, 2002.

Henkes, K. *Chester's Way*. New York: Mulberry, 1997.

Henkes, K. *Sheila Rae, the Brave*. New York: Mulberry, 1996.

Henkes, K. *Julius, the Baby of the World*. New York: Mulberry, 1995.

Hesse, K. *Out of the Dust*. New York: Hyperion Books for Children, 1997.

Hest, A. *The Great Green Notebook of Katie Roberts: Who Just Turned 12 on Monday*. Cambridge, MA: Candlewick, 1998.

Hutchins, P. *The Doorbell Rang*. New York: Greenwillow, 1986.

Ketteman, H. *Bubba the Cowboy Prince: a Fractured Texas Tale*. New York: Scholastic, 1997.

King, M. L. *I Have a Dream*. New York: Scholastic, 1997.

Kline, S. *Marvin and the Mean Words*. New York: Putnam, 1997.

Lester, H. *Tacky the Penguin*. Boston: Houghton Mifflin, 1990.

Littledale, F. *The Boy who Cried Wolf*. New York: Scholastic, 1987.

Marshall, E. *Fox at School*. New York: Puffin, 1983.

Marshall, J. *Red Riding Hood*. New York: Dial, 1987.

Marshall, J. *George and Martha Back in Town*. Boston: Houghton Mifflin, 1983.

Maynard, C. *Micro Monsters: Life under the Microscope*. New York: Dorling Kindersley, 1999.

McGovern, A. *Stone Soup*. New York: Scholastic, 1986.

Medina, J. *My Name is Jorge on Both Sides of the River*. Honesdale, PA: Wordsong/Boyds Mills Press, 1999.

Moss, M. *Amelia Writes Again*. Berkeley, CA: Tricycle, 1996.

Parks, B. *Junie B. Jones Loves Handsome Warren*. New York: Random House, 1996.

Pinczes, E. *100 Hungry Ants*. New York: Harcourt Brace, 1997.

Rathmann, P. *Officer Buckle and Gloria*. New York: Scholastic, 1995.

Rockwell, T. *How to Eat Fried Worms*. New York: Franklin Watts/Scholastic, 1973.

Ross, T. *The Boy who Cried Wolf*. New York: Puffin, 1985.

Rowling, J. K. *Harry Potter and the Sorcerer's Stone*. New York: Scholastic, 1998.

Ryan, P. *Esperanza Rising*. New York: Scholastic, 2000.

Sachar, L. *Sideways Stories from Wayside School*. New York: Avon, 1993.

Salinas, B. *Los Tres Cerdos/The Three Little Pigs: Nacho, Tito, and Miguel*. Alameda, CA: Piñata Press, 1998.

Schwartz, A. *In a Dark, Dark Room*. New York: Harper & Row, 1985.

Schwartz, A. *Scary Stories to Tell in the Dark*. New York: Harper & Row, 1981.

Scieszka, J. *The Book that Jack Wrote*. New York: Viking, 1994.

Seuss, Dr. *Green Eggs and Ham*. New York: Random House, 1960.

Silverstein, S. *Where the Sidewalk Ends*. New York: HarperCollins, 1974.

Soto, G. *Chato's Kitchen*. New York: Putnam, 1995.

Spinelli, E. *Somebody Loves You, Mr. Hatch*. New York: Simon & Schuster, 1992.

Steig, W. *Spinky Sulks*. New York: Sunburst, 1991.

Taylor, M. D. *The Gold Cadillac*. New York: Puffin, 1998.

Thaler, M. *The Librarian from the Black Lagoon*. New York: Scholastic, 1997.

Thaler, M. *The Teacher from the Black Lagoon*. New York: Scholastic, 1989.

Van Allsburg, C. *Jumanji*. Boston: Houghton Mifflin, 1981.

Van Allsburg, C. *The Sweetest Fig*. Boston: Houghton Mifflin, 1993.

Weinberger, K. *Cats That Roar*. New York: Scholastic, 2002.

Williams, L. *The Little Old Lady Who Was Not Afraid of Anything*. New York: HarperTrophy, 1988.

Wood, A. *Heckedy Peg*. New York: Harcourt Brace, 1987.